BREADCRAFT

Also by Alan Littlewood:
Careers in Catering

Breadcraft

A Master Baker's complete guide to home baking

with best wishes

Alan Littlewood 20/3/99

Alan Littlewood

Allison & Busby
published by W H Allen & Co Plc.

First published in 1987 by
Allison and Busby,
A division of W H Allen & Co Plc
44 Hill Street, London W1X 8LB

Set in Palatino by Input Typesetting Ltd

Printed and bound in Great Britain by
Adlard & Son Ltd, The Garden City Press

British Library Cataloguing in Publication Data:

Littlewood, Alan
Breadcraft.
1. Bread
1. Title
641.8'15 TX769

ISBN 0–85031–738–X

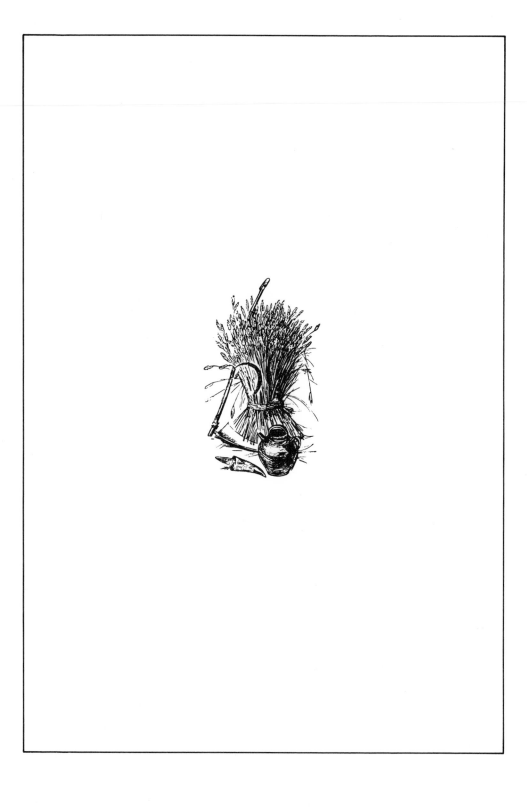

8

Contents

Acknowledgements

Just as a loaf of bread is characterized by the individual's use of methods and materials, so this book is the result of imprinting my personality upon the knowledge and experience I have been blessed with.

My grandfather started the small family bakery at the beginning of this century. As a child I remember every inch of the walls of the shop other than the display case was covered with framed diplomas won in open competitions, for confectionery, pastries, and mainly for bread. Until the mid 1930s, Grandad's name dominated the business and then, in the years after the war, my father became increasingly involved. I was apprenticed to my father, and learnt most of the basic skills in those early years.

By the time I was eighteen I was collecting diplomas, even though the shop walls were full! Trained to excel, the covered walls seemed to indicate that I needed new fields to conquer. I studied the technical side of the craft in detail at Leeds College of Technology and then baked my way round half the world in the Merchant Navy before managing in turn a biscuit bakery, a small meat pie factory, a leading confectionery bakery and a pastry kitchen for a top hotel. I also worked under top craftsmen in order to learn specific skills, each for six to twelve months until I had learnt what I could.

I wrote articles on all my experiences for the bakery trade press, and taught part time in the local bakery school, and so learnt early on not only how to find out what I wanted to know but also how to pass it on to others. My first full-time teaching post was a further attempt to learn by working under a real Master, the late W. J. Fance. Will Fance taught me to teach and to write: he was a master at both. I moved up the teaching ladder to Ealing to work under Dennis Searle and A. S. West, two different but superb men of bakery education, before becoming the Bakery Division Head at Ealing College.

I have been helped by every person I worked with as well as those worked for, by every student I have taught, every bakery book I have read, all the firms that supply bakers with raw materials, and those organizations in which technical knowledge is shared.

I enjoyed many years of teaching amateur bakers as well as professionals, and it was one of my enthusiastic students, Miss Rosamund Wade, who opened the way for this book through enthusiasm for my presentation of baking skills. I would like to thank Rosemary Rowett for typing, and my publishers for much helpful advice during the final stages of preparation.

Briefly, that sums up the ingredients of the book. The method of putting it together is much more complex and a study for others. Suffice it now to say that as a warm new loaf is presented to a family for them to cut, eat and enjoy, so I offer this volume in the hope that it will bring joy in the reading and much satisfaction in the practice of this ancient craft.

Bread — An Introduction

In the modern world we are so often filled with amazement by new technologies and sciences that it is easy to take for granted those older skills and techniques often referred to as crafts. In fact today it sometimes appears that the more immediately useful a task is, the lower the status it is accorded. It was not always so.

The discovery of fire and its control, the development of the mystic mixing of the pulped seeds of certain grasses with water and their subsequent cooking on a hot stove came early in human civilization. How early is not known, but it is difficult to imagine the existence of any real form of civilization before the cultivation of some cereal for making some kind of bread or porridge.

The tasks of making fire, pounding grain and cooking these early flat grass-seed cakes would have belonged to the wives and mothers, assisted by daughters. Men would perform the more dramatic tasks of hunting for meat and skins, and defending themselves from, or attacking, neighbouring villages and tribes. As it became more possible to cultivate the grain, and thereby improve its quality, some of the men would devote themselves to the arable side of agriculture, using stalks to make straw for cattle fodder (as well as bricks, mats, roofs, etc.), and harvesting the grain for their womenfolk to make into bread. The grinding of the wheat, its mixing into dough and forming it into flat loaves was therefore a part of the work of women. The whole of this lengthy process is still undertaken today by women in many parts of the world, particularly in rural areas of India.

The sort of bread produced would no doubt seem very tough to our modern "spoilt" palate; and it was possibly in primitive times that wives discovered that such toughness could be softened by mixing in some of the fat from a recently killed pig and moistening the dough with milk rather than water.

There is no way of knowing exactly how and in what order the various breadmaking arts were developed. Early bread would have been made from wheat, oats, maize, barley, or any combination of these and other long-forgotten grasses, until gradually the cereals most suitable came to the fore. We do know, however, that the making of wines and ales is about as old as the making of bread; so, at least to some extent, fermentation was understood in deepest antiquity.

It must have early become known that dough allowed to "rest" before cooking turned out bread less hard than that baked straight after mixing. Perhaps some ingenious wife, acknowledging her husband's fondness for the wine pot or brewing ale, decided to try using some of the contents in her dough — imagine her surprise to discover that while waiting for the fire to get hot her dough actually increased in size. And if the finished article did not produce the same effect as consuming an equivalent quantity of wine or ale, was the bread not much more pleasant to eat? Moreover, her cakes were bigger, lighter, from bouncier, bonnier doughs. Wine, it seemed, could do something for dough that could not be done by milk or water alone.

Not to be outdone by this feat of discovery, Mr Early Man must have watched his wife pounding meagre handfuls of grain between two stones and decided that his donkey or slaves could pound much more grain much more quickly with some kind of a machine. And having developed a primitive prototype of the mill, capable of grinding more flour than his own family required, his services could be extended to cover the needs of some of his neighbours.

But, as with most discoveries, there were bound to be set-backs. The ground barley meal or oats, when treated in just the same way as the wheat, would not rise. In fact only wheat and, to a lesser degree, rye would rise with the yeast from the wine vats. This revelation must have increased the value of wheat, and its demand, accompanying the developing taste for risen loaves.

As the economic division of labour became more established, especially among the rich, the baking of bread became more of a male preserve. The Egyptians learned their baking from the Babylonians, and it is in ancient Egypt that we find the first references to baking as a profession, the bread and cakes either being fried in hot fat or baked in an oven. Frequent references to bread and cakes are also found both in ancient Greek writings and in the Bible.

The spread of the Roman Empire and, later, of Christianity brought with them an interchange of baking knowledge and skills. The Romans, who never conquered Scotland, thought its inhabitants barbarians because they ate oatmeal porridge and not wheat bread. (The Scots have since become so civilized that they probably make the best wheat breads in the world, though they still consume huge quantities of oatmeal porridge!) In the Roman Empire, the professional baker was a most respected member of his community, a position he was to hold, with odd exceptions, until the industrial revolution.

The industrial revolution hit at all crafts, but its direct effect on the baking of bread was somewhat delayed, partly because of the complexities of the process (dough is not an easy material to push through machines) and partly because of a public that refused to accept second-best mechanically produced foods while there were still enough small bakeries prepared to keep prices competitive — something which they could do so long as labour was cheap and hours of work lengthy. Eventually, the shorter hours and better pay of other industries drew many people away from craft baking.

Those who stayed were often the ones who were devoted to the craft itself. Many of them looked forward to a day when customers would be prepared to pay enough for them once again to be able to make goods of the high standard of former years. But many others, less sentimental, were not averse to cutting cost and qualtiy in order to price down to a public that wanted above all the fruits of affluence and cared little about "ordinary" things such as bread. However, people longed for "good old-fashioned bread" until the generation that had been accustomed to it died out. Their daughters complained, while buying increasing quantities of characterless loaves which might as well have been sliced putty or cotton wool — but they still went on buying it. Yet here and there a craftsman would prove that there is still a good living to be had from making good bread, though unfortunately many more demonstrated that it was even easier if you sold bad bread.

However, until the last generation at least, the rural housewife had never ceased making her own bread at home. A generation now almost dead of country home bakers had carried the old craft from mother to daughter, with many families of craft bakers passing their more refined craft knowledge in city and country shops from father to son.

My own knowledge of breadcraft began when I was a small child helping with the tins and then being apprenticed in my father's bakery, which he had purchased from his father. My fascination for bread has been with me from as far back as I can remember; and marrying a farmer's daughter let me into some of the secrets of the country kitchen. Comparing notes between these two approaches to good breadmaking has been one of my strongest interests.

There are, of course, few secrets these days about baking (or very much else) to the enquiring mind. But not so long ago, certainly on occasions in my own lifetime, much of the detail which contributes greatly towards good craftsmanship was kept pretty well hidden.

In the days of the powerful guilds, such as those of the White Bread Bakers in London (who never got on with the Brown Bread Bakers, until in 1569 Queen Elizabeth I signed a charter uniting the two, under the domination of the former), the secrets of the ancient craft of baking were closely guarded, and passed on to apprentices as an initiation into the guild as well as an education.

Recipes, until very recently, were sold for sometimes large sums of cash and were widely regarded as the most important factor in the making of good bread. If success was not achieved, this was blamed on a faulty recipe, when often enough the baker's skill must have been the main influence.

There is, then, some advantage in setting such a value on what people know, since it becomes respected by those who do not know, and obtains a certain mystique. However, mystique can be used as an excuse to cover up false knowledge or to hide real ignorance. The development of technical education for bakers (which dates back to the 1880s in some regions) helped a great deal towards opening up a knowledge of breadmaking to all whose chose to enquire. Another contributing factor is the more recent shortage of skilled staff which, along with the expansion of book publishing, has disseminated knowledge of the craft fairly widely. The trouble, though, with telling everyone your secrets is that after a while people don't want to know them, and after a bit longer there is no one left to tell. In this way crafts die.

While industry may find scant time to produce the bread of yore, and scope (except in notable exceptions) for enjoying the craft profitably becomes less, many people — working shorter hours, being better housed and often boringly entertained — are once again turning to those crafts which were the sole delight of their forebears. Few of them really want to go back to grinding wheat with a pestle and mortar (unless out of curiosity) but many would like to find out something of the joyful feel of warm, live, silky dough, and the homely smell of baking coming from the oven, not to mention the incomparable taste of real, good, honest, fresh bread.

Breadmaking is a science, a craft and an art. Practised as a hobby it is eternally satisfying because it is such a joy in itself: the mixing and handling of the combination of living ingredients; the careful fermentation; the baking of lovely crusty rolls or handsome, crisp cottage loaves. . . . But there is also the further attraction that baking-day could once again present a family with the simple luxury of excellent home-made bread.

Unfortunately, what is often liable to happen is that a frustrating day is spent producing an apology which sends the erstwhile enthusiast rushing out for another sliced loaf, determined never again to be lured into meddling with the fermentation of dough. For this business is not like frying chips or serving up a soup from a packet. It is not even like making a cake, for which a few simple instructions will often suffice. It is more like the very raising of life itself. Something magical, like some sort of age-old witchcraft, seems to be involved.

After a while, the lure of making bread will creep back. It is a compulsion from the far distant past to find again the real pleasure of this strange process by which a large portion of humanity has been mainly fed since the dawn of its history. There is something inherently satisfying about making bread, something as fundamentally human as getting washed, or sleeping at night, or having children.

If it is no longer feasible to get the secret in person from one's mother, or grandmother, or great-grandmother, then at least modern science has answered a few of the most pressing questions relating to this mysterious process, and this does make it possible to indicate more clearly what is going on and what needs to be done to ensure good results.

Some of the details may appear somewhat complicated at first, but once they are understood the door is open to almost any innovation. And herein lies the most important secret of breadmaking: if you understand the process, you do not even need a recipe to achieve successful results. Recipes are like notes of music; you use them to interpret what someone else has composed. Well-tried compositions are usually good compositions, but to be able to create your own as well as repeat the idea of others is to master an art, not just to follow a craft.

Breadmaking is basically about understanding the interaction of four ingredients: flour, salt, yeast, water. It takes nothing else but a baker to make these into excellent bread. Nothing else.

The Store Cupboard

The kitchen store cupboard — usually the same place as the larder, except in old country houses — used to be of considerable size, for inside it and the larder large amounts of food were preserved or stored. Our larder at home was used for salting pigs and for making butter and cheese, but little of this is done today and most of its stone shelves are filled with bottles of home-made wine and beer. Situated down a short flight of stone steps, under the kitchen, the larder is always cool and sometimes cold. Foodstuffs are kept in store cupboards on either side of the steps, where it is cool yet not so damp as the "cavern" below.

As a result of the modern tendency to buy food in small but frequent quantities, more recent houses have small kitchens without much storage room, though it is gratifying that architects are once again designing kitchens of a size to accommodate the increasing activity that goes on in them. The kitchen is the workshop of the house, the heart of a home. Not only are housewives more interested in the culinary arts, but so are large numbers of husbands. Co-operation in the kitchen is a growing part of leisure, rather than the cause of constant drudgery. In recent years, many people have taken to brewing their own beers and wines, and making bread is (as it was centuries ago) a natural extension of this interest in fermentation.

The necessary breadmaking ingredients are few and inexpensive, and there is no need to keep large stocks of them. One of the main advantages of making bread is precisely that success depends not on unfamiliar or costly materials, but upon the correct use and appreciation of a few humble items. Bread is the plain background for other more exotic foods. It is the ideal accompaniment to almost any dish, yet nutritionally is more valuable itself than it is given credit for in times of affluence. Inexpensive meals with good bread can be a treat, while a banquet served with poor rolls becomes a bore.

The majority of bakeries lack the time to make many of the varieties which would suit all tastes and complement each kind of food perfectly. Yet selecting the right bread for a meal should be as important as choosing the wine, or the ideal herbs for a soup.

Since we have established that making bread requires a supply of flour, salt, yeast and water (and occasionally one or two other things which are present in most kitchens anyway, such as fat, sugar, honey, milk or eggs), an introduction to these main items should make our task more interesting as well as more successful. For success will depend on our use of them, and much of the enjoyment will derive from understanding what is happening to them.

Wheat

Wheat is by far the main cereal used in breadmaking. There are many varieties, and the ones used for making bread flours today are of a much better quality than those used in earlier days. It is from the seed of the plant that wheat flour is obtained.

Wheat is grown in many parts of the world — from India to Canada, from Egypt to Australia — and the wheats from each climate are in many respects very individual. Since the harvests naturally occur at different times of the year, the flour miller has a problem working out how to blend various wheats to make a flour of anything like similar quality throughout the year. That nowadays this can be done is a tribute to modern technology.

It is important to understand what we do when we cut down this plant, since in so doing we are interfering with a natural process; wheat does not grow for the purpose of feeding people, any more than people live in order to fertilize wheat.

The seed or grain consists of an outer skin (actually several layers of skin) called the bran, which encloses a small germ (nucleus of the new plant) and the endosperm. The bran is a protective coating, like the shell on an egg. The endosperm is composed largely of starch and protein and is provided as food for the germ, just as in a fertilized egg the white is for the yolk (chick).

Left to itself and unharvested the seed would ripen and the starchy endosperm would be changed into sugars and other foods to feed the germ, which would fall to the ground and send down a root in search of more food, and a shoot into the air, which would become the new plant. Many complicated changes are involved during this process, but only two of them concern us at this stage. The first is the change from starch to sugar, brought about by the action of something called diastase, and the second is a softening of the protein caused by protease. Both these "ases" are enzymes — complex substances which cause changes in other things.

When the wheat is harvested there is a lot of starch in the endosperm but very little sugar. There is also much protein which can be quite tough. But these mysterious little enzymes are present ready to start work when the change comes. Outside they wait for autumn warmth and rain. Harvested, they will still be waiting for warmth and moisture, for they do not change their life potential by being cut down.

So the life is still in the grain when it arrives at the mill, but untapped, unused, awaiting its chance. And the miller intends to keep it that way. For if the harvest was late, or wet, much wheat would be sprouted, and would not be of much use for breadmaking.

Flour

From his supply of wheat, the miller can make any of a number of different kinds of flour. The main ones used in breadmaking are wholemeal, white flour and germ meal. Wholemeal makes use of the whole of the grain, white flour is milled endosperm, and germ meal is 75 per cent strong white flour mixed with 25 per cent cooked, salted wheatgerm. Germ meal is not generally available to the public, but the other flours can be readily obtained.

One kind of flour never used in breadmaking, of course, is self-raising flour; and whatever flour is used ought to be bread flour, and can usually be bought as such.

It is sometimes possible to buy loose flour from a baker's shop, if bread is baked on the premises, and this is the best flour for the purpose. Some bakers may resent what seems to represent a potential loss of custom, but most appreciate that few people actually make all their own bread, and that the increasing interest in bread helps everybody in some way.

Salt and water

Modern science and technology has solved many of the problems faced by our parents and grandparents in baking and cooking, not least of which is the fact that most of our ingredients are purer than those used in the past.

Water is obviously necessary for breadmaking, dough being a mixture of flour and water, although the water may come in the milk or eggs rather than from the tap. The main hazards in domestic water were formerly connected with unsuitable materials being used for storing and piping it, but these days we need have few doubts about the possible health risks of water. Although its hardness varies from one part of the country to another, the effect of this on bread is slight. Our own water at home on the farm comes by modern polythene piping from an ancient spring on the edge of the moor. Drunk neat it is as good as wine, very soft and slightly acid. It makes the most beautiful tea on earth but needs a little hardening when used for brewing ale. For bread, it appears to be no better or worse than town-supply chlorinated soft or hard water.

The salt used today is similarly easier to handle without fear than that available in former years, and any proprietary cooking salt is much easier to deal with than the hard lumps of rock salt which once had to be pounded into powder first.

Salt is always used in breadmaking. Its absence causes the bread to be almost unpalatable except to those who, through strict salt-controlled dieting, have become used to it made in this way.

Salt is a chemical — a fact which needs to be stated in view of much emotional criticism of the use of chemicals in food production. It is essential to human health; and, probably because of its essential nature, it has an unusual quality. In amounts so small that it cannot itself be tasted, salt has the effect of heightening or increasing the flavour of other ingredients in almost any type of food, whether sweet or savoury. However, only in the case of very special kinds of bread would one wish to be aware of the presence of salt. For normal purposes, the object is to bring out the distinctive flavour of the bread, not to smother it. There are in fact other important reasons for including salt in bread, which will be discussed later. For the present, suffice it to say that this is the third of the four major actors in the drama of breadmaking — and flour, water and salt are the original ingredients used to make the first bread.

By adding to these three some fat, milk and a little sugar it is possible to make unleavened bread of the type baked many thousands of years ago taste much more palatable.

For making dough, flour will take just over half its weight in water, and a useful guide to the amount of salt required is to use a quarter of an ounce to each pound of flour (or 15 grams per 1,000 grams of flour).

Yeast

In the packet of dried yeast, or the bit of putty-like live yeast purchased from the delicatessen or a local baker, there is no visible indication of the forces contained within.

Yeast is in fact a single-cell plant, oval in shape like a plum, but no more than $1/3000$ inch long (about 5 microns). Although these little "plants" have been used for thousands of years in the production of ales and bread, until the time of Louis Pasteur (from whose name is derived the term "pasteurization") the fact that fermentation was caused by the action of such organisms was not known.

The yeast cell consists of a cell wall surrounding a jelly-like protoplasm in which floats a nucleus. There are other details, of course, but this rough description is enough for now. Notice that this three-part system is much the same as that met with in the wheat grain, the egg (which I used to illustrate it) and the plum; with skin, flesh and stone.

Bakers' yeast and brewers' yeast are of a similar type, but that used for making wine is usually of a different variety. Yeast is found in the "wild" state floating in the air, and also in soil. It settles on sugary materials such as fruits (causing the bloom on grapes or jams, for example). It normally reproduces by each cell dividing into two, which happens whenever there is enough moisture and food and a suitable temperature.

The main food of yeast is sugar. There are several different kinds of sugar, but all can be classified as either complex (known as disaccharides) or simple (monosaccharides); the only complicated thing about this is the names. Sucrose is the chemical name for ordinary household sugar, and whether extracted from cane or from beet it is exactly the same when refined. Sucrose is a complex sugar, and the importance of this in the present context is that yeast can only feed on a simple sugar. The yeast cell wall is so fine that sugar dissolved in water cannot pass through.

Why then, you may well ask, is it that household sugar can be fermented by yeast? Because yeast, the clever little bug, carries on the outside of the cell wall an enzyme called invertase which changes complex sugars into simple sugars that can then pass through the wall. Once inside, the simple sugar (invert sugar) is digested by another enzyme, zymase, which turns it into alcohol and carbon dioxide gas.

Actually it is not quite as simple as that, but this pattern is sufficient for our purpose: sugar is changed to invert sugar outside the cell, absorbed by it and when inside changed to alcohol and carbon dioxide gas, which are then passed out of the cell. In breadmaking we are not really very interested in the alcohol except in so far as its development affects flavour; but we are interested in the production of gas, which pushes up the loaf and therefore provides the much-desired lightness.

Yeast, being alive cannot be used in indiscriminate amounts. The quantity needed for any dough varies depending on the temperature of the dough and the length of fermentation time. You can calculate these yourself, but for most of the recipes in this book already calculated yeast quantities will be given.

If at all possible, fresh live yeast should always be used. It can often be bought from a baker's shop where bread is baked on the premises. Fresh yeast used to be available from breweries, for during brewing large amounts of yeast are produced which are later taken out of the ale. There are fewer breweries about today, but anyone who can get hold of a little yeast from one will find that it adds a wonderful flavour to the bread.

You can make your own yeast, either as a barm or by using that which settles out if you brew your own ale with live yeast. The doughs are never quite as light, but the flavour may to some extent compensate for this. A barm is similar to a ferment (see page 70) but using less yeast and much more time. Part is used for making bread, part is topped up with everything except yeast, to reproduce for the next day.

Failing any of these sources of supply, dried yeast on the market can be used. My prejudice for a lively fresh yeast may be old-fashioned, for good loaves can be made with the dried product, using about three-quarters the amount shown in the recipes.

All yeast should be stored cool (not frozen) and used as soon as possible after purchase. An ordinary refrigerator is all right, but keeping time cannot be definitively stated, since one cannot know how fresh the yeast is when bought. If it is fresh it should "break" easily. When old it may either turn very dark and dry or, if kept damp, become more like putty, being pliable with no break.

Magic powders

Good bread can be made from flour, salt, yeast and water. The only other essential "ingredient", a wise old baker told me, is craftsmanship. It is obvious what he meant, even though craftsmanship is really an umbrella for all the other things that may be helpful, from control of temperature and timing to humidity, amount of handling and possibly, on occasion, small quantities of what are often called "bread improvers".

More than a century ago, a leading baker called Walter Banfield found that by mixing equal weights of plain flour and lard (or cooking fat) well beaten to a cream, and then beating in the same quantity of pure honey, he produced a creamy mixture which considerably improved bread quality when added to dough instead of the equivalent amount of fat and sugar in the normal way. For best results, the improver should be stored in a jar for about two weeks before use. It can be used with any bread recipe at the rate of 1½ oz (45 g) improver to replace ½ oz (15 g) each of fat and sugar.

Flour will normally contain enough natural wheat sugar to feed the yeast during short fermentation times and more can be produced from its own starch for longer processes. A small addition of sugar, malt extract, syrup, glucose, treacle or honey makes sure, though too much will change the bread's character.

Consistency of quality is especially important in commercial bread; flour (being a natural product) may vary from one batch to another, and yeast needs more than just sugar in order to work at its best. Minute amounts of ammonium and potassium sulphates and phosphates can, however, make a considerable difference to fermentation and thus to the resultant bread. As the amount required is so tiny, what better way to measure it correctly than to mix it with either some flour or some of Walter Banfield's Improver? Specialist suppliers began marketing brand-named bread improvers to the industry, to be used along with flour, salt, yeast and water according to makers' instructions. While earlier bakers had also used mashed potatoes (potato starch) in small quantities to aid fermentation, by the 1950s soya flour was being used instead, having a bleaching (whitening) effect on dough, as well as helping the development of gluten. Soya flour became the "carrier" for trace mineral yeast foods.

Crumb softness, aided by up to ½ oz (15 g) fat per 1 lb (480 g) flour, was found to benefit by smaller additions of emulsifiers such as a glycerol monostearate, even with less added fat. So this also could find its way into bread along with the "improver".

In 1961 the Flour Milling and Baking Industries Research Association at Chorleywood in Hertfordshire brought out the Chorleywood Bread Process (CBP) of breadmaking. For this the dough received a measured amount of energy input using a specially constructed high-speed mixer. A small addition of fat was essential, as were minute quantities of antioxidant, either ascorbic acid or potassium bromate. The process made it possible to produce commercial bread without a period of fermentation in bulk. The powder could be added to a proprietory improver, saving time at the weighing stage and making weighing much more accurate than is possible with such small quantities. There was and still is much debate on the effect of the no-fermentation process on a bread's flavour, and longer processes are returning to favour.

Fermentation, originally achieved by time only, could be achieved by mechanical development in the CBP, or by chemical means in a process called the Activated Dough Development system (ADD). This requires the addition of a very small quantity of L-cystene as well as oxidants, in place of a special mixer. Added to a proprietory improver, this method could even be used in domestic situations.

Were it not for further developments in the existing field of bakery research, government and EEC pressure on flour millers to use more home-grown (English) weak wheat could have led to a serious deterioration in bread quality. Contributions of the above and other minute additions to dough have made it possible to produce acceptable bread from flour which not many years ago would have been considered totally unsuitable for this purpose. This is especially so with wholemeal bread, since it contains much less gluten, the valuable wheat protein, which holds in the aerating gas and so enables wheat bread to rise. Without much modern research of this kind it is unlikely that the recent fashion for brown and wholemeal breads, regardless of nutritional theory, would have really taken off. Even what we ought to eat needs to be palatable if it is to be accepted by more than an enthusiastic minority.

For the in-store bakery and hot-bread shop, where fresh bread is produced at the point of sale and bakery craft skill may well not be available, these "magic powders" are sold already mixed in the flour. By controlling the recipe through use of the pre-mix in the bag, and the method by using automatically controlled mixing machines, the skill required in the bakery can be reduced to a minimum. Craftsmanship and technical understanding are hardly necessary in such a system. They go back to the supplier of the machines and the bag of mixes.

The home baker has no such technical backing. Craftsmanship becomes more important. Lack of "magic powders" in the home means that home bread will rarely be as light as bought bread, and its main advantage will always be that it includes a crucial ingredient less evident in many commercial undertakings: love. Anyone who has ever considered the place of bread in the Holy Communion service will know that this "ingredient" really makes all the difference.

Equipment

Most of the equipment essential for making good bread is to be found in the average kitchen, but one or two items that are not always present deserve mention.

You will need a firm baking table on which to work the dough, one with a smooth, clean surface and the strength to stand up to some hammering.

One or more handbowls will be needed to take the rising dough, of course, and a couple of clean tea-towels for covering it while it is standing.

A good pair of scales is necessary, since consistently good results will depend on all the ingredients being weighed; measuring alone is not accurate enough. The weights for recipes in this book are given in metric as well as imperial.

Just as accurate weights are important, so is working at the right temperature. Many home bakers try to make do by guessing this, but no professional would feel absolutely confident to make such a judgement without a thermometer. Special dough thermometers can be bought, though a clinical thermometer will be adequate provided it registers at least as low as about 50°F and is not used for anything above its maximum reading.

Two or three bread tins will be required for ordinary tin bread, but many types of bread can be made using trays or cake tins.

Then there is the oven — for nothing are we more dependent on modern manufacturers than this. It is often the least reliable part of the process, although a few useful tips may help in its mastery:

• Do not make more dough than your oven will bake at one go.

• The ideal oven has no hot or cold areas within it but holds the same temperature steadily throughout baking. Your oven should be equipped with a thermometer so that you can see at a glance what its temperature is. Regulos are all very well but they do not tell you everything; however, in case you do not have a thermometer and cannot get one fitted, we will manage by giving regulo approximations with oven temperatures. Oven thermometers don't always accurately show the temperature inside anyway, but with experience you can get to know how far out they are.

Apart from these items, little else is required except a couple of wire trays on which to cool the bread, an eggwash brush for washing the tops of certain loaves, a sieve to sift the flour and, of course, some handy holders for pulling out the bread without burning yourself.

Any other odds and ends will be mentioned along with the relevant recipes. The only other important thing to remember from first to last is that self, kitchen and all utensils must be kept *spotlessly clean*, not only out of personal pride and for the sake of the health of those who will eat what you bake but also to ensure the best possible results.

Weights and Measures

In a large industrial bakery where doughs are made using 560 lb of flour and over 30 gallons of water, the weighing of ingredients is very carefully controlled. Part of the reason for this is connected with keeping costs down, for the profit rate on bread is not high, as anyone will soon realize if they tot up the cost of making a couple of loaves at home. The money saved is not much, if you include the cost of oven heat, and will soon disappear altogether if you try to cost in your time and labour. Any saving will be in other more expensive foods by having nicer bread and so eating more. The same money saving would come by finding a good baker and buying much more bread.

However, if it is important to weigh correctly because of the cost factor, the main reason for such careful weighing is still because if you don't you will be taking too many risks with your ingredients. Good baking begins with good and careful weighing.

All the recipes are given in both imperial weight and metric, but the following may be useful for converting any other recipes.

16 oz = 1 lb
1,000 g = 1 kg
1 g = 0.035 oz
approximately 28 g = 1 oz
500 g = ½ kg = 1 lb 1½ oz
5 fluid oz = 1 gill
4 gills = 1 pint
2 pints = 1 quart
4 quarts = 1 gallon
8 pints = 1 gallon
10 lb of water = approximately 1 gallon
1 lb of pure water weighs 1¼ lb.

Temperature

Centigrade = $5/9$ (Fahrenheit −32)

Fahrenheit = ($9/5$ Centigrade) +32

Oven Temperatures

	°F	°C	Regulo
Cool	300–400	150–200	3–4
Moderate	400–450	200–230	4–6
Moderately hot	450–475	230–250	6–8
Hot	475–500	250–270	9

The 'Hovis' Sandwich Girl - A Genuine 'Hovis' Sandwich is Highly Recommended.

How to do it

Having introduced the *dramatis personae*, we can now look briefly at the drama.

There is little to be gained by repeatedly describing the same procedure with each recipe, so below is the basic method which is applicable to many different kinds of bread; it is not the only method, but it will help us better to understand the job we are about to do. It is known as the straight dough method, because all the ingredients are mixed into the dough in one stage.

Take note right away that all ingredients should be weighed, rather than just measured. Further, if you are to improve your bread with practice it is a good idea to record in a notebook a few vital details of each dough made — for example, the times and temperatures of each stage, and your (and your family's) remarks about the result.

The first thing to do is to take the temperature of the flour and write it down. Then there is a little sum to do — nothing like higher mathematics, but it is necessary for getting the dough made at the correct temperature.

The dough temperature we require is 80°F (27°C). Double this dough temperature (160°F) and subtract the temperature of the flour just written down. Say the flour was 65°F, then the result will be 95°F and this is the temperature to take the water. Write it down. (This is easy with an all-water dough, but when using milk and/or eggs the whole liquid content should also come to this figure.)

Now for the method as used in a recipe, for two wholemeal tin loaves, with weights given in both imperial and metric.

Wholemeal Bread

1 lb 0 oz	wholemeal flour		460g
¼ oz		salt	7g
½ oz		honey or treacle	15g
11 oz	water		310g
1 oz	lard		30g
1 oz	yeast		30g

Straight dough method:

Sieve the flour; probably the wholemeal will not all go through the sieve, so what does not go through must go over. The object is not to make it finer but to make sure there are no lumps or bits of string or paper in it, as may occasionally happen. Sieving is a good habit to acquire.

Weigh the salt and lard, and along with the flour rub them together on the table (not in a bowl) using clean hands; a wooden spoon is not needed.

When the mixture is nice and crumby, take a measure of water and get it to the correct temperature, then weigh the required amount. Weigh the honey or treacle into this and mix together. Finally weigh in the yeast and mix that into the water too. There should now be two mixtures ready and even, one of dry ingredients and the other of liquid (or liquor). Note that we did *not* cream the yeast with the sugar (honey and treacle are both largely invert sugar). Most cookery books from Mrs Beeton on have carried the misleading instructions about mixing yeast with sugar; in fact this does no good at all and it can damage the yeast to meet so heavy a concentration of sugar.

So, dissolve the sugar in the water first, then mix the yeast into this. Provided that the kitchen is reasonably warm, this liquor could be allowed to stand for about ten minutes just to get the yeast busy. But it is not essential and if there is any risk of chilling it is better to dough up straight away.

The first part of dough-mixing is rather like mixing cement. Make a hole about ten inches across in the pile of flour, using the flour as a wall all the way round. Pour in the liquor; it should not run out of this hole. Then, bit by bit, draw in the flour and stir it through with the wide-opened fingers of one hand until you get the consistency of thick custard, surrounded by the remainder of the flour.

With both hands palms upwards and fingers open, push the rest of the flour through the "custard" and shake it up lightly until all the flour is wet. If it feels a bit stiff at this stage (getting it right first time can only be learned with experience), add a little more water. Flour does vary in the amount of water it will take, and wholemeal anyway will take more water than white flour. Do make sure the water is warm.

All the dough ingredients are now mixed together, but this combination of materials is not yet dough. The mixture has to be *kneaded* to make it into dough.

Kneading is really stretching and tearing. Part of the dough is held with one hand, while the other hand stretches and tears the remainder from it up the table. Hold the dough with the left hand and with the heel of the other hand push out part of the dough. Then turn it around and repeat; make sure that all the dough receives this treatment, with no odd scraps collecting outside it.

Kneading should take from ten to fifteen minutes. It should be quite hard work when you first do it, and the more thorough the kneading, the better the bread. My grandfather used to mix by hand 280 lb of flour this way every day; the little doughs we are concerned with should present no real problem.

There are two reasons for not using a machine to do this. First, no machine on the market for household use has a kneading action (which is not the same as mixing). Secondly, in hand-kneading you are experiencing the feel of the changes taking place in the dough; you are getting to know the dough. Kneading is one of the joys of the task, one of the ways through which you stamp your own personality on your bread, making it as individual as your signature.

When the dough is smooth and silky, and prefers to stick to itself rather than your fingers, scrape it off the table and shape it into a smooth ball.

Warm the bowl, take the temperature of the dough and write down the time and the temperature. Place the dough in a bowl and cover it with a damp cloth.

Now the theory is that this dough should remain at 80°F from when it is mixed until it goes in the oven, but maybe your dough did not finish up at exactly 80°F. There is bound to be heat loss from water on the scales and from the dough on the table. Maybe after working out the water temperature next time you should add a couple of degrees. Or perhaps a bit more care or speed in handling is called for. The weather can also affect things, as can kitchen draughts and suchlike hazards. Of course the ideal of 80°F is not often achieved, but to have the aim clear is useful; writing down the actual temperatures and times makes better control possible, so that each batch of bread is an improvement on the last.

Place the bowl of dough somewhere where the temperature is as near 80°F as possible and where there are no draughts. The damp cloth should be laid over the bowl, not touching the dough (otherwise it will stick to it). This is to prevent the dough forming a skin from the air. Let it sit there untouched for forty minutes, during which time it will grow to two and a half times its original size.

Then take it out of the bowl and on the table hammer the gas out of the dough, before balling it up again and putting it back to rest for a further twenty minutes. This is what is called "knocking back". It is a good time to give the dough another five minutes' kneading if you are really keen on getting the best out of it. But remember that the next twenty minutes start when the dough is back in the bowl and under cover.

During this last twenty minutes there is time to make sure that the oven is heating up properly and to prepare the tins. The oven will need to be hot, about 480°F–500°F, and preferably it should have been hot for a while before the bread goes in.

Two small loaf tins should be thoroughly cleaned (but not washed, unless absolutely necessary) and thinly greased all over the inside with lard or the fat from a joint of meat (dripping). Dripping taken from the Sunday roast, put in melted, is well recommended because, when applied thinly over the inside of the tin, it puts a lovely crust on the bread.

Since we are trying to keep the dough warm, the tins ought to be warmed (not hot), and this can be achieved by putting them in the oven for a very short time just before the dough is ready to take.

When the dough is ready, take its temperature and record this, then divide the dough into two. This is best done by weight, since any difference will affect the baking time. The dough should be light and full of bubbles of gas. It will stretch more easily than when it was made or when it was knocked back.

The dough now has to be moulded (shaped) for the tins. It is at this point that the shape and appearance of the finished loaf is largely fixed, so care must be taken that it is done well.

First shape the two pieces of dough, one in each hand, into round balls; this can be done quite lightly. Next, taking them one at a time, and with the crease facing upwards, roll them up like Swiss rolls. Make sure that no air gets rolled into them. Lay them on the table with the crease upwards again and cover them with a damp cloth for five minutes.

Then turn them the other way (pointing towards you) and pin them out again, this time also widening them to the length of the tin, and roll them up quite tightly. At this stage there should be no gas left in them; if there is, roll them over straight away again. If they do not get enough pressure they will be loose and flabby, whereas they ought to be firm and smooth. If the moulding is too tight the surface will tear, and it will be necessary to allow another five minutes' rest and then start again.

When moulded, the loaves should be placed straight in the tins, crease to the bottom; lay a damp cloth over them and write down the time. The loaves should of course be placed in a warm place (80°F). The table can now be washed, along with all the utensils used.

The time from placing the loaves in the tins to putting them in the oven is called "proof". We have a potential problem here in that the loaves would reach the damp cloth covering them before they are ready; so just before they get that high the cloth must be removed. However, since proving the loaves dry may cause "skinning", a way of keeping the air around them damp has to be found. Some people put the loaves in a large biscuit tin or similar container, laying the damp cloth over the top. This is fine. Similarly, you could use a box or a small wooden cupboard, covering the opening with a damp cloth, or putting a bowl of hot water inside and closing the door. In this way you can also keep a check on the proving temperature by putting the thermometer beside the loaves.

All our checking of times and temperatures, nevertheless, will not alter the fact that we cannot say in advance precisely how long this proving is going to take. The object is to get the bread when it is just coming up to its largest size. Too soon or too late and the loaves will not be so good. The length of time will vary according to the type of flour, the wheat it came from, the handling of the dough and the working temperatures. Experience is the main judge, and it will depend on each person getting used to the effects of their own way of working.

This dough will probably take about half an hour to prove. It should be about twice to two and a half times its original size before going back into the loaf tins, and if you press the surface slightly it should spring back when the fingers are released. The loaves are then ready to go into the oven.

Without knocking them, place them in the middle of the oven, not touching each other but as far from the sides as possible. Make sure there is plenty of headroom for further rising. Ideally the oven should start at 500°F and, as soon as the loaves go in, be allowed to drop slowly to 480°F. As some ovens, particularly electric ones, are a bit dry, it may help to put a tray (such as a meat-roasting dish) full of hot water at the bottom, to give the bread some steam.

As soon as the bread is in the oven, close the door, note down the time and temperature of setting, and leave well alone.

After twenty minutes you can remove the tray of water, and, although it is best not to touch the baking bread at all, if the heat is uneven and there is more baking at one side or other (or more on the back than front) turn the loaves around. This must be done carefully to avoid any bumping or knocking. Then shut the door again as soon as possible. Whatever colour the loaves are, they are not yet ready, they will take half an hour to bake, maybe even thirty-five minutes; so if they are dark at twenty minutes it means either that there is too much top heat or that the oven is too hot.

Try them at the half-hour by knocking a loaf out of its tin and tapping its underside. If it sounds hollow it is ready. If not, put it straight back for a few minutes.

When the loaves are ready, set them out of the tins on a wire tray, spacing them apart so as to let the steam out, and let them cool before further touching. They will be best to eat between one and twelve hours old. Don't forget to write down the time they came out.

So that's it then. It will probably take from two and a half to three hours altogether, later coming down to just over two hours with a little practice. Once you are confident of and know what you are doing, the total working time is only about half an hour. It takes many of us no less time to go out and buy a loaf.

Baking times

Ovens vary considerably, so there is no substitute for getting to know the one you use. In many ovens there is more heat at the sides or back and less in the middle. It is therefore sometimes necessary to turn the tray round when the goods are half-baked. If the top tray bakes quicker than the one below, it may also help to exchange the trays during baking. Goods in one part of the oven may need less time than those baking in another part of the same oven.

The shape and content of the goods themselves will affect the baking time, as well as the size of each item.

Generally, the higher the sugar content, the lower the baking temperature and the longer the baking time. For this purpose, by the way, sugar includes malt, milk (lactose), glucose, honey, fondant or syrup.

As a rough guide, it is usual to bake a loaf scaled at 1 lb or (or 450 g) for 30–35 minutes and a 2 lb loaf (900 g) for 40–65 minutes.

You can tell when a loaf is baked by knocking it underneath. If it sounds hollow, it is ready; if it sounds "dull", put it back for a while longer.

Baking times are not often given with the recipes in this book, since they can be misleading. You will need to take into account your own oven and the other variables. A clock is not the most reliable guide to baking.

This all goes to show that, as with other aspects of breadmaking, the actual baking isn't always boringly automatic!

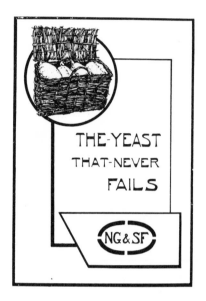

The Straight Dough Method

Keep this page open when making bread by this method. (Place it under clear polythene to avoid getting dough over it.) It summarizes the main details in a concise form.

1. Wash your hands. Set the oven.
2. Weigh all ingredients except sugar, yeast and liquids.
3. Rub weighed ingredients together.
4. Take temperature of this flour mix and write it down.
5. Double the required dough temperature, subtract flour mix temperature and write down this resulting temperature.
6. Weigh water and liquids at the temperature just recorded.
7. Weigh sugars and mix them into liquid.
8. Weigh yeast and mix it into liquid.
9. Make a bay in the flour mix.
10. Pour in the liquid, and bring in enough flour to get a smooth "custard" consistency.

11. Shake through the rest of the flour until it is all wetted.
12. Adjust water if necessary.
13. Knead well for 10–15 minutes until smooth.
14. Take dough temperature and record this and time.
15. Put dough to prove in a *warm bowl* under a damp cloth.
16. Knock back dough and knead again at proper time. Record time and temperature.
17. Prepare and warm loaf tins and check oven temperature.
18. At proper time, divide loaves and mould and tin them.
19. Prove carefully as near as possible at the dough temperature required, and not too dry.
20. When loaves are ready, put them in oven, spaced so that heat can get round. Write down time and temperature.
21. When ready (sounding hollow when tapped underneath), take loaves out of tin. Write down time and temperature.
22. Cool baked loaves on a wire tray.
23. Complete record sheet.

The Record Sheet

Wholemeal Bread

Time		Dough Temperature
10.00	Dough made	78°F
10.40	Knocked back	77°F
11.05	Taken	77°F
11.15	Tinned	–
		Oven Temperature
11.45	Set in oven	500°F
12.18	Taken from oven	480°F

Date

What it was like

When mixing	Slightly stiff. Added 1 oz warm water.
When moulded	Nice smooth dough. Lovely.
When set in oven	Bold, lovely loaves.
When taken out	A bit dark. Oven too hot. Bake cooler next time.
When cut	Sliced nicely, but not thin as so fresh. Leave longer before cutting.
Buttering	Spread easily.
Family taste	Smashing! Crust a bit hard.
Own Remarks	Too many big holes. Funny shape. Mould more carefully. Otherwise happy loaves!

Brown or White?

It matters little at this stage whether you have just read through the last bit or have actually made the bread, as long as the intention is there. What matters now is that we accept that this is not a once in a blue moon landing adventure, but that we are jolly well going to learn to master this business. And once in the grip of its fascination there will be no holding back.

Take a look at the example record sheet, which gives a rough idea of what yours might look like. From it you will see just how valuable a record can be, for it shows just what to watch most carefully with the next dough. So next time you make bread the first thing you do is browse through the most recent record sheets, and so easily remember the points to watch. In this way one gets to know the odd distinctions of one's own kitchen, especially the oven, and also the effects of one's own way of working.

The basic tasks involved in the straight dough method are summarized in order on a separate page for easy reference while you are actually making the bread. It obviously cannot include all the information but it will make a handy reminder.

Immediately after making the first dough, or merely reading about the first dough, is the ideal time to take a slightly more detailed look at what has been done. And the first question that will probably be raised is: "Why make such a great fuss about weights and temperatures and timetables?" The reason is because so many things which can go wrong — things which used to be blamed on the weather, the gods, or it being one of those days — can be prevented, but only by taking care over such details.

There is another reason. One very quickly tires of a hobby which can be mastered in five minutes. Much of this recording business is intended to show how one can learn more about the fermentation and baking of bread. Looking at what we have just done, for example, presents many interesting questions.

The salt is always mixed into the flour, and the yeast into the liquor, because these two must not come in direct contact with one another since salt kills yeast just as surely as it kills slugs when highly concentrated. In the dough itself salt has an effect on the fermentation, for it prevents the yeast from racing away out of control, in other words it steadies the yeast.

Also mixed with the flour is the lard. Any fat will do, but lard is probably best from the flavour point of view. It is used in small quantities in bread of the type we have been discussing, and the quantity given is a maximum. It improves the crumb of the bread in this quantity, but more would change the type of it altogether. Fat also in this small quantity makes the bread lighter, and brighter in colour, although it tends to clog the yeast action a little and so, as with the salt, is mixed in the flour away from the yeast.

Before the dough was mixed, a solid mix and a liquid mix were prepared. These two being well mixed separately makes the mixing of the dough easier. Also making the "custard" makes it easier to get the flour through smoothly with less work, and then wetting all the flour gently helps prevent an accumulation of scrappy bits which would be difficult to work through the dough.

The question of kneading is not so simple. I have a collection of cookery and bakery books, some of which date back several centuries in content, if not always in printing date, and though all recommend and describe this kneading action as necessary when making bread, not one attempts to explain why. It was obviously accepted from early times that kneading was essential for good bread, and hand-kneading is certainly a much older skill in most of our families than, say, writing.

We have already mentioned that wheat contains quite a large amount of protein along with the starch in the endosperm, all waiting for germination to use it as food for the new plant — waiting, that is, for warmth and moisture to change its form. When we make dough we provide both.

This protein is the body-building part of the wheat. In the flour it is dry, of course, and when wetted it forms a wet mixture which holds the other materials of the dough together. But besides doing this it actually begins to change its form, taking in a large amount of water and forming a substance we call gluten. Gluten is very important, for without it there would be no risen bread as we know it. Only two cereals contain protein which when wetted makes this gluten: wheat and, to a lesser extent rye. This is why a risen loaf cannot be made with the other cereals, although they each contain protein.

Gluten is a rubbery substance which stretches like elastic and tends to spring back. When it is first made, by wetting the flour, it is tough and breaks easily. But with stretching and tearing it obtains a springy texture which enables it to hold in the gas during fermentation, and stretch whilst the dough rises. This is why the kneading action helps to get the dough in good condition for holding the gas to be produced by the yeast.

Another natural question to ask is why we have to go to the trouble of leaving the dough to rise (twice) just in order to knock the gas out again. Why not just put it straight in the tin and let it rise once only where it matters? Because when dough is first made the gluten is tough. The rest allows it to soften out a little, for this is where the protease already in the flour gets busy. So in fact the fermentation of bread has little to do with letting it rise. We are more concerned with getting it into the right condition to stretch with the gas during proof.

However, other things are happening during this time as well. Diastase is changing a little of the starch into sugar, which the invertase on the yeast is then changing into invert sugar, digesting, and passing to the zymase for conversion into carbon dioxide gas and alcohol. The gas is bubbled into the dough, causing it to stretch with the softening gluten, until, if left long enough, the gluten bubble would burst and the gas escape. To get the lightest possible loaf we must therefore have enough of this gluten-making protein already in the flour, and a suitable amount of both protease to soften it and diatase to provide later food for the yeast. We must also by kneading and fermentation get the gluten in absolutely the best condition to hold all the gas to be produced by the yeast.

With so many things going on in the dough all at once, things which at no stage can the eye see, a sort of second sight needs to be developed to sense what is happening and to get them all proceeding at the right rate.

If the dough is made much hotter than 80°F, the yeast will work much faster, as will these little enzymes. However, other enzymes not yet intro-duced will get busy as well, producing off flavours ranging from vinegar to rancid butter and sour milk. If, on the other hand, the dough is made too cold, it will move much slower, and produce a bread with different characteristics altogether, about which more later.

There are enzymes in the bran as well as in the endosperm, but all the gluten-making proteins are in the endosperm. So if we remove the bran (in other words, buy white flour), we shall have a higher proportion of these vital proteins. You would then expect to be able to make much lighter bread; and, of course, you can.

There is another reason why white bread is lighter than brown, and that is because the bran is rather like sawdust shavings. It cuts through the gluten like a lot of little knives, and so prevents it from holding quite so much gas as it otherwise might.

Considering the practical difficulty of separating the skin from the inner endosperm, it is indeed surprising that white bread has been known for so very long. White bread was the food of the wealthy for centureis when the poor could only afford brown, and it is a bit ironic that in our age it costs more to buy brown flour than white even though so much surplus bran goes back to the farms as cattle feed. But such ironies are part of the price of industrialization. Stone-grinding of wholemeal flour has become a small-scale specialization, catering for a particular public, although there has been a modest increase in recent years.

From Roman times the coarser bran was sieved out of the bread of the wealthy and for centuries brown-bread bakers were of a different profession from the bakers of white bread, the former selling to the poor. It was not until the late sixteenth century that Queen Elizabeth I of England granted a charter to the Worshipful Company of Bakers of the City of London, legally binding the White Bread Bakers and the Brown Bread Bakers into one Livery Company.

The increasing demand for a whiter and whiter loaf (especially during the 1950s when the maximum possible amount of endosperm was used in white flour) led to big improvements in the milling of white flour in the post-war years. This was followed by some very heated arguments about the nutritive value of white bread versus brown, and the argument, often heard before the war, has continued on and off ever since. Like many other arguments it is a bit of a waste of time when everyone is emotionally on the boil, but tempers seem quiet enough by now to say something about the business without too much fear of being shot at by either side. There are few topics that I can remember being the subject of such controversy, or about which so many silly things have been said and written by people who ought to know better.

The first thing to emphasize is that bread, be it white or brown, is a very valuable food. Now we have already seen that the food of wheat is really in the endosperm, which provides both starch (an energy-giving food) and protein (a body-building food). But what is the bran made of?

The bran is Nature's protection for the food of the new plant. It is tough and fibrous, and formed largely of cellulose. It is a substance which is not digestible by the human system; the human body can do nothing with it. The fact that horses, donkeys, sheep, cattle and goats can convert it into useful food is neither here nor there in this argument. For people, it provides no food, or extremely little.

What then does it do? It is certainly true that removing the bran means removing some valuable minerals and vitamins. However, in most Western countries, vitamin and mineral supplements are added to white flour in order to ensure that the nutritive value is no longer lower in white bread than brown.

Bran has been described as something like sawdust. Recent research has emphasized the value of fibre in the diet, and more of this is available in the bran than in the endosperm or germ. However, it must be emphasized that white bread is a source of dietary fibre, containing about a half of the dietary fibre present in wholemeal bread weight for weight (see Table IV page 145).

After many tests and a good deal of research it has been well established that along with a normal balanced diet the best bread to eat for most people is that which they like best. The main finding is that almost all people would lead healthier lives if they at least doubled the amount of bread they eat.

One final argument needs to be disposed of, and that is the one which says in effect that wheat is Nature's gift to man, and should be eaten without additions or subtractions — in other words the wheat, the whole wheat and nothing but the wheat. If this is because you like that kind of bread better, all well and good. But wheat is not Nature's gift to humanity. Wheat is a plant, a seed from which a new plant should grow. We only have the use of the wheat by interfering with a natural process and harnessing it to our own use. Further, if we want the whole wheat, why not take the stalks as well? Then we would really have some roughage!

The subject of flour additives other than those mentioned above for nutritional purposes is another matter, and one which probably does need a more careful watch, as is the subject of chemical fertilizers and their effect on both the flour and bread, and on the soil. But there will be little success in the demands for better control of the food we eat until there is a lot less emotional shouting and a bit more accuracy brought into the discussion.

A much lighter loaf can be made with white flour rather than brown. It is better for this to buy a breadmaking flour, definitely not a self-raising flour and preferably not an all-purpose flour. All-purpose flours are low in protein; they have to be of average quality to do many different kinds of jobs and therefore are really not particularly good for any, and are certainly not the best for making bread.

The method will be "straight dough", just the same as with the wholemeal. The tins ought to be a little larger because of the extra lightness we expect, and the hand-kneading will need to be if anything even more thorough, because of the extra gluten to be made. Otherwise everything is very much the same.

There is one improvement that can be made at this stage, however, provided you are becoming more confident about holding the dough at 80°F throughout. If the yeast quantity is cut in half it is possible to increase the fermentation time to double that used before. This can be done next time with the wholemeal if you wish, and in fact can be done with any of the recipes. It does not work the other way because you cannot make good bread in any less time. But the increase of time should improve the loaves quite a lot. It depends on how you organize your time in the kitchen, for it will not take any more time actually working the dough. And of course although other times will be doubled, like the fermentation and proof, the proof *may not* need the full double time, and the baking time will not be altered.

What difference will this extra time really make? Well, there will be a better softening of the gluten, giving a better shaped loaf. More natural sugar will be produced and fermented in the dough, and therefore give a better flavour, but it all depends on keeping the temperature right throughout a longer period of time. If you can do that and don't forget anything, the next bread will be better whether it is white or brown. Times for both amounts of yeast are shown in the recipes on pages 48–9, so now we can take a look at white tin-breads and one or two other varieties, all using the straight dough method already described, and all requiring the precautions mentioned earlier, just the same as with the wholemeal.

Tin Bread

Not, I must say, so-called because of any metallic ingredient, nor due to any similarity. Tinned bread would be a more accurate term, but is known widely in England as tin bread. In Scotland and Ireland the term is pan bread, and in either case the term denotes that the bread is made in a container of some kind, usually a bread tin or bread pan.

Tins for making bread come in many shapes, besides which many kinds of tins can be used which are not designed primarily for this purpose. The capacity of the tin is important, as this will govern the quantity of dough which can comfortably be baked in it, and this in turn will affect the baking time. It may take some experimenting to find the right amount of a given kind of dough for any particular tin, but getting this right will greatly improve the shape of the finished loaves.

There are two main kinds of tin loaf: the open tin and the closed tin. The open tin is able to rise above the tin during the last stage of proof and that stage we call "oven spring". Oven spring is the extra rising that takes place after the bread has gone into the oven, but before the yeast has been killed by the heat and the crust fixed.

In the case of the closed tin loaf, the bread is either baked under the tin, or the tin is covered with some kind of lid during baking. Obviously it is going to be even more important to get exactly the right amount of dough in a closed tin than an open one. Not enough and you will get a poor-looking loaf, but even a little too much will find some way of getting out.

There are a series of complicated calculations which can be used to work out the right amount of any kind of dough for a tin. However, since dough weights for commercial bread are fixed by law, and tins are made to suit the legal weights, they are not often used in industry. As the bread made for home consumption (including that used in catering, provided the bread is sold in quantities less than a loaf) is not governed by these regulations, some calculation is called for. But it is easier to arrive at the right amount of dough by experience and old-fashioned trial and error. A good rough guide is that the dough, if well made, will probably multiply its volume by about two and a half times, so use about two-fifths of the capacity of the tin in dough. This will be adjusted with richer types of dough.

Tins of a variety of shapes will enable one to produce many kinds of bread from the same dough. And if that sounds like cheating, do remember that the shape of the tin will influence the baking speed, the area of the crust, and the size and convenience of the slice. So in fact different shapes usually do mean different types of bread. Do make sure that the sizes of loaves at any one baking are equal, so that they bake at the same rate.

Further variation can be introduced by using tins of different materials, for this governs to some degree the speed at which the heat penetrates the loaf. With a new shiny tin this will be very rapid and harsh. Such a tin really needs to be burnt off by greasing it inside and out lightly and baking it empty in a *cool* oven (about 360°F) for up to, say, five hours. The best bread tins are nearly black, or certainly a rich bronze colour.

They should not be dirty, but this may help to explain why we earlier mentioned a preference for dry wiping over washing. Washing affects the surface.

Plant-pot bread

Bread can be made in many other containers besides bread tins and cake tins. One of the most popular loaves of a generation ago was made under a plant pot. This made a marvellous loaf because of the slow bake, and had many of the advantages of the old solid brick oven. The hole enabled surplus steam to get away so that if the dough was right it came out just the shape of the inverted plant pot. If you want to try this, make sure you use a real plant pot, not one of the more recent polythene or plastic things — which of course melt or burn on heating, producing a most unpleasant odour, a puff of blue smoke, a mess in the oven and the most horrible-tasting loaf you ever threw away!

Mentioning the use of clay may suggest other ideas to you worth trying out. Of course these containers need a good greasing, and it is a good idea to flour them as well with the same kind of flour used in the dough, be it white or brown. This gives the loaf a "homely" surface especially on a wholemeal or wheatmeal loaf, and helps to get the bread out of such a container.

The surface of the pot, after greasing well with lard, could be dressed with any number of other things, however, to give a different finish and crust flavour to the bread. You could use coarse bran on a white or brown loaf. (One way to get bran back into a white loaf is to stick it round the crust. Then you have all the lightness of white bread, plus the flavour of the bran!) Or you could be more adventurous and use oatmeal, porridge oats, semolina, ground rice, yellow maize flour, or even crushed-up break-fast cereal or dried coconut. All you have to do is thoroughly grease the pot and pour in the dressing. Run it all over the inside by turning the pot, then tip out all that is not still stuck to the sides of it.

The dough pieces after fermentation are shaped round, placed on a warm, greased tray and covered with the plant pots. The pots should not then be moved until baked, but it is possible to tell when the dough is almost at the top (about ½ inch away is about right) by gently letting a light stick (say a match) drop through the hole. See how far it drops before kneading the dough. This wants doing when the loaves are nearly ready for the oven. There is no need to lose any matches in these!

Baking takes longer than for ordinary bread because the heat has to get through the pot as well. It will probably take some practice to get the knack of making these loaves really well, but if you have a yen for the old-fashioned flavour, then here it is. For it, use the recipes for straight white or wholemeal bread, or for farmhouse bread.

Other possible substitutes for tins are mentioned later. Meanwhile, let's get back to our bread dough. . . .

Wholemeal Bread

1 lb 0 oz	wholemeal flour	460 g
¼ oz	salt	7 g

½ oz	honey or treacle	15 g
11 oz	water	310 g
1 oz	lard	30 g
1 oz	yeast	30 g

Straight dough method. Dough temperature 80°F. Bulk fermentation time 1 hour. Knock back after 40 minutes. Yield two tin loaves. Mould into 1 lb bread tins or as required. Baking temperature 480°F–500°F. Baking time 30 minutes.

White Bread

1 lb 0 oz	white bread flour	460 g
¼ oz	salt	7 g
½ oz	sugar	15 g
10 oz	water	300 g
1 oz	lard	30 g
1 oz	yeast	30 g

Straight dough method. Dough temperature 80°F. Bulk fermentation time 1 hour. Knock back after 40 minutes. Yield two tin loaves. Mould into 1 lb bread tins. Baking temperature 480°F–500°F. Baking time 30 minutes. (To yield one large loaf, mould into one large tin and bake at 480°F–500°F for 40 minutes.)

White Bread (longer fermentation)

1 lb 0 oz	white flour	460 g
¼ oz	salt	7 g
½ oz	sugar	15 g
10 oz	water	300 g
1 oz	lard	30 g
½ oz	yeast	15 g

Straight dough method. Dough temperature 80°F. Bulk fermentation time 2 hours. Knock back after 80 minutes. Yield two loaves moulded into 1 lb bread tins, or one large loaf. Baking temperature 480°F–500°F. Baking time 30 minutes for small loaf or 40 minutes for large loaf.

Farmhouse Loaf

1 lb 0 oz	white flour	460 g
¼ oz	salt	7 g
1 oz	honey	30 g
10 oz	milk	300 g
2 oz	egg (1 whole egg)	60 g
1 oz	lard	30 g
1 oz	yeast	30 g

Straight dough method. Warm milk to required temperature. Whisk the egg into the milk along with the honey (or golden syrup, if you don't have honey) and then yeast. Dough should be softer than for previous breads. Dough temperature 80°F. One hour bulk fermentation. Knock back after 40 minutes. Mould up as before, then press flat into warmed, greased oven glaze or other shallow pie-dish. Press out or pin out to fit. Prove fully out of draughts, then dust top lightly with flour and make ½ inch deep cut lengthwise with a razor blade down the middle of the top. Don't knock, for it should be very light. Bake at 460°F for 45 minutes. The result should be a beautiful loaf indeed.

Note the lower baking temperature necessary for the higher sugar content. The crust colour of all bread depends upon the sugar content, since it is largely caused by the caramelization of sugar; so more sugar means lower temperature and longer baking. The extra enrichment tends to clog up the yeast, and this can only be eased by using a softer dough. So the richer the dough, the softer (or slacker) we make it and the cooler we bake it.

This farmhouse loaf is supposed to remind you of the country kitchen, hence the loading of milk, honey and eggs. Milk contains its own natural sugar, a complex sugar called lactose, and this one is not fermentable by yeast at all. Therefore it stays in the loaf to provide colour and flavour after fermentation. For a better flavoured loaf use milk that is a little sour.

Semolina is easily obtained in grocers' shops. It is unmilled coarse endosperm and can be used to give a more "country" texture to your farmhouse loaf by substituting 3 oz of the flour, so the total is still 1 lb.

Wholemeal flour may have difficulty in holding up that amount of enrichment and part wholemeal part white flour would manage better if you want a brown farmhouse. If you do, use treacle instead of honey, increase the milk to a soft dough and leave the egg out altogether. Dust with the same wholemeal before cutting. The recipe and method for this is given below.

Wholemeal Farmhouse Loaf

1 lb 0 oz	wholemeal flour (or 12 oz wholemeal and 4 oz white flour)	460 g
¼ oz	salt	7 g
1 oz	treacle	30 g
11 oz	milk	330 g
1 oz	lard	30 g
1 oz	yeast	30 g

Straight dough method. Dough temperature 80°F. Bulk fermentation time 1 hour. Tin as Farmhouse Loaf and bake at 460°F for 45 minutes. Flavour can be improved by adding a pinch of cardamom and a pinch of cinnamon and/or nutmeg to the flour. Try it.

How Long Will it Keep?

Not very long if you eat it, of course. And if it is as good as we hope then it will be eaten pretty sharply. Bread was never a food to buy or make for the week, and if at all possible it should be bought or made, and eaten, fresh and often. Why anybody should wish to keep bread for more than a couple of days I can't imagine. All the doughs mentioned are of a size that will be eaten quite quickly. So why does it matter?

Maybe you don't eat much bread. But bread is still the cheapest source of energy and protein by far. Eating more bread therefore cuts the cost of other foods without reduction of quality. Of course you can double the size of the recipe provided your oven is big enough to take it. But the bread will not probably be quite as pleasant after two or three days. "The trouble with making your own bread," I have heard it said, "is that you eat so much of it." Is that a trouble? Or is it not rather a compliment?

But, however well you manage it, on some occasions there will be bread to keep. Bread correctly mixed, fermented and baked fully will keep much longer than that which is not so well made. Stale bread is unpalatable and dry; but very little of this dryness is caused by moisture drying out of the bread. It is due to a shift of moisture between the starch and the gluten, a shift which can be prevented by deep freezing the bread after cooling it but before it is twelve hours old. It should, of course be fully thawed before use. Bread which is beginning to stale can be rejuvenated by putting it back into the oven for about ten minutes. In this way the moisture shift is reversed. This is also what happens when toast is made.

Bread which is heavily enriched, such as the farmhouse loaf, seems to dry out quicker, but makes better toast for up to about a week or ten days after baking. The smaller kinds of bread, such as rolls and buns, will dry out much quicker than the larger loaves.

Apart from the problem of staling, which is largely solved by making the bread properly and eating it fairly soon afterwards, there is the problem of mould. Bread will grow mould if it is too damp, especially if it is also warm. To prevent this bread is cooled all round, quickly but without draughts, then stored cool in a bread bin (*not* wrapped in polythene or wax paper, containers which can only keep mould-damp inside).

One other way to prevent staling, and keep bread for lengthy periods of time, is to make it into rusks. In this way the bread is completely dry, and therefore is quite different in character from fresh bread. As long as they are kept dry, rusks keep indefinitely.

What Went Wrong?

The actual work involved in making a loaf or two of bread is really very little, apart from the already emphasized need to watch times and temperatures. Even people who spend a lifetime making bread cannot expect to achieve top standard all the time, but by examining the results of each batch it is possible gradually to find ways to eliminate most of the beginner's faults. Apart from it being useful to diagnose the causes of one's own baking faults, you will be better able to spot what is wrong with bread you see in the shops, and eventually to recognize easily a good loaf if you do go out to buy one.

Ugly shape: more often than not caused by bad moulding. This is a problem for the inexperienced, for good moulding (shaping) only comes with practice. All the gas should be expelled and the surface smooth but not torn. Other causes of bad shapes may be too stiff a dough, oven heat not sufficiently even, wrong oven temperature, not enough steam in the oven, too little or too much fermentation (check times *and* temperatures), or handling the loaf too much before it is cool.

Loaves with flying tops (top crust harshly breaking from the loaf): can be caused by not long enough proof, too much heat in the oven, or bad fermentation control.

Too much colour on the top crust: could result from too long in the oven but if the times given are held to this is not likely. It could result from too much salt or sugar; try cutting the sugar down or even out completely on a short dough process. Or it could be that the oven is too hot.

Crust pale and anaemic-looking: the dough has probably had too much fermentation, possibly because it was too hot. This could also be caused by forgetting the salt (which allows the yeast to gobble up all the sugar) or be the result of a skin forming during proof (due to lack of moisture in the air around the proving dough).

Spots on the crust: usually caused by the loaf having been moulded on a table which is not perfectly clean, or from using unclean tins. Drops of condensation water in the oven could, however, cause this.

Big holes in the bread: could mean too much proof (which gives a hole just underneath the top crust), that the loaf has been knocked before being put in the oven, or has been moulded from dough with a skin, or too much flour, or on a greasy surface.

Tough, open, honeycomb-type texture: the result of too much water. Badly mixed dough will cause holes, but also practically every other fault in the book. There is no excuse for it after all that kneading. A very thorough kneading is particularly important when you are mixing a long sponge with a fresh dough.

Bread dries too quickly: it has probably not been fermented for long enough, or it may be short of salt or baked in too cool an oven.

This list includes most of the faults commonly met with by beginners (and others), though there are many other possible imperfections that can occur in bread, and not all of them are fully understood. Being aware of what can go wrong should certainly help prevent the most gruesome examples of the above faults. Obviously it is largely a matter of degree, since many of these defects may be present to some extent in most loaves, and the baker will be constantly trying to eliminate them, with the aid of the regularly kept record-sheets.

Old-fashioned Wheatgerm Bread

It has long been acknowledged that wheatgerm contains many valuable nutrients. Being the essence of life of the grain, the romantic have been inspired to make exaggerated claims for wheatgerm's medicinal value. The same philosophy motivated cannibals to believe that in eating their victims, they were able to digest and so possess their noble qualities.

In the 1880s attempts were made to produce a bread enriched with wheatgerm. As the germ was extracted from white bread, it could be fairly readily purchased from white-flour millers. The earliest wheatgerm breads were made from a proprietary flour containing 75 per cent very strong flour (because the germ has no gluten) and 25 per cent cooked, salted wheatgerm. The cooking helped the flavour and the keeping; the salt also acted as a preservative.

The germ was carefully roasted; a time-consuming and technically difficult process. To reproduce the best quality germ bread of the late nineteenth century in the home involves us in problems beyond the reach of most of us today. However, present-day wheatgerm bread must contain at least 10 per cent added processed wheatgerm, and may contain up to 5 per cent soya-bean flour.

My family were national champion bakers of wheatgerm bread from before the First World War. The following recipe gives as near as I can achieve a reproduction of the best flavoured and most nutritious germ-meal loaf.

Wheatgerm Bread

(a)	7 oz	wheatgerm	200 g
	½ oz	salt	15 g
	1 lb	water	460 g
(b)	1 oz	yeast	30 g
	1 oz	water	30 g
(c)	1 lb 5 oz	strong white flour	600 g
	10 oz	water	280 g

Stir (a) in a saucepan over heat until it cooks and thickens. Cool to 120°F then add (b). Warm the water (c) to 110°F and mix in. Finally mix to a warm dough with the strong white flour. It will be quite soft and should be beaten and stretched vigorously for at least 5 minutes. Immediately it is kneaded, divide into three loaves, shape and drop into three 1 lb loaf tins that have been warmed and well greased. Prove for about half an hour then bake at 460°F–480°F for about 30–35 minutes. The oven should also contain a dish of hot water to increase humidity.

If you can get hold of it, use Canadian flour for the strong bread flour for a bit more lift, but if you do, the mixing must be more vigorous.

Milk Bread

Milk bread is bread made with full-cream milk in place of water. It is not necessarily better because of this, but it ought to be very different. For one thing, the colour is richer. Also, the bread is very slightly sweet and you can taste the milkiness. The farmhouse bread already mentioned is an all-milk bread, but this is not its main feature and does not show up so clearly.

Milk has several interesting effects on dough. Part of the natural protein (casein) in milk is apt to make the dough "bound" and therefore heavy. This effect is countered by the butterfat of the milk, so milk bread should never be made with non-fat (or skimmed) milk. Anyway, it is not really milk bread if it is not made with whole milk.

When making milk bread, it is necessary to use more liquid than when using only water, partly to free the dough from the binding effect just referred to and partly because milk is not, of course, all water. The dough should be quite soft (but not sticky after kneading) for a good milk loaf.

It is possible to make a perfectly good milk loaf, in the same way as any other bread, by the straight dough method. The milk will need to be warmed before use, but it gives a better flavour if it has not been above about 110°F until baking.

Something else worth remembering is that milk bread should be baked in a *slightly* cooler oven (about 460°F–470°F) for a little longer than an all-water bread. This is because sugar is what causes a crust to go brown and the milk's natural sugar (lactose) is not fermented by yeast, so is present throughout the process.

Apart from remembering these few points, all you have to do is use milk instead of water in the first two recipes (pages 29 and 48) to produce satisfactory milk bread. However, while there is nothing wrong with using the straight dough method like this, a much better milk bread loaf with a nicer flavour can be made using a sponge and dough process. It takes no longer but it gives the flavour a better chance to grow.

Sponge and dough

The dough is mixed in two stages. The first stage uses all or most of the liquid, the yeast, those ingredients which help yeast get busy, (such as sugar), those which assist the flavour, and some flour: make a paste with these and allow it to ferment. Then make up the dough as before with this "sponge" and the rest of the flour to which has been added the ingredients which earlier would have held up the yeast, such as the salt and any fat. This method can be used to make any kind of bread, but it is particularly suitable for milk bread because of the fine flavour built up in the sponge. This is further helped if the milk used is just slightly souring.

All the precautions mentioned previously — about controlling the time and temperature and having sufficient damp over the dough during fermentation and proof — apply equally to all breadmaking, of course. So, without going through it all again, it should be stressed that good bread will only be made where constant care is taken over such details.

Milk Bread

Sponge	10 oz	milk	280 g
	½ oz	sugar	15 g
	1 oz	yeast	30 g
	10 oz	flour	280 g
		a pinch of nutmeg	

Weigh the milk and pour it into a bowl big enough to take a full-size dough. (The doughs in these recipes are mostly of approximately the same size.) Place the bowl in a larger bowl, the sink, or other vessel of hot water, and stir the milk slowly until it is 108°F. At this point take it from the hot water.

Dissolve the sugar in the milk, and then mix the yeast through it and throw in a small pinch of nutmeg to heighten the flavour. Sieve the flour, pour it on the top of the liquid and stir it through. This is best done with the hand. Open all the fingers and beat the mixture vigorously for 3 or 4 minutes to make up the gluten and knock in some air. Then scrape the bowl down and clean the mixture off the hands. Cover with a damp cloth and allow to ferment for 1 hour at 80°F.

During this time the yeast is able to work much faster than in an ordinary dough, the gluten gets a good stretching, and the natural flavours of the flour and milk are able to develop well along with those of fermentation.

It may help to give it another beating after 30–40 minutes, although this is not essential. The main thing is to time the whole period of the sponge to 1 hour.

During this time (after writing down the time the sponge was made and the temperature of it) the two loaf tins are prepared, and the dough ingredients weighed up and rubbed together. A bay is made in these, on the table, just as was done with the straight dough, although the extra milk is kept in a measure or a cup separate from the rest.

Dough			
	2 oz	milk	60 g
	6 oz	flour	170 g
	¼ oz	salt	7 g
	½ oz	butter	15 g

If the sponge is a bit on the warm side (over 80°F) when it is ready to take, the extra milk can be taken cold. But if the sponge has lost heat, warm the milk. Warm the clean, lightly greased loaf tins, but don't let them become hot.

Pour this second lot of milk straight on to the bubbling sponge and work it through with the hand. This will knock out much of the gas in the sponge. Then pour the liquid into the bay, and mix and knead into dough in the usual way. As soon as the dough is well kneaded (and it should be lovely and smooth and soft and silky) divide it straight away into two equal loaves and mould them up in a warm (80°F), moist atmosphere.

When they are light and bold, and ready for the oven, make five cuts about ¼ inch deep along the length of the top of each with a razor blade before setting them in an oven at 460°F. They will take about 35 minutes to bake, after which they should be taken from the tins and placed on a wire. Brush the tops with milk as soon as they come from the oven for a rich, soft brown crust and a handsome sunburnt finish.

If well made, this bread will keep for days, and make marvellous toast for up to about a fortnight if given the chance. A similar loaf can be made with wholemeal flour instead of white, using treacle or malt extract in place of sugar. In all the recipes using white flour there is some improvement in both flavour and fermentation if you use white honey (as white as can be bought) in place of sugar. For apart from the natural flavour added, honey is largely already invert sugar. Much the same could be said for golden syrup or malt extract, but in most cases sugar is the word used in the recipes.

Just a word of warning, however, about malt extract. Malts vary, and those made for brewing beer are very high in diastase, too high for normal bread. They can be used provided you first heat them gently to about 180°F to destroy much of this diastase, before adding to the water (never to the yeast). The other point, of course, is that having so inactivated the malt, it ought not to be used afterwards for brewing beer.

There are lots of other shapes for the milk-bread dough, besides the one I have described, and each can produce a handsome loaf.

If after moulding the dough is rolled out like a thick rope to just over a foot in length, and then twisted into an "S" shape and placed in the tin in this way, a scroll finish is obtained instead of the cutting.

By dividing each loaf into several equal-sized pieces, shaping them round, and placing them in a round cake tin or loaf tin, a further shape can be made, or the loaf can be shaped round, placed in a round tin, flattened down with the hand just a little, then proved and cut with a razor blade or a pair of scissors just before going in the oven. The blade can be used to cut squares on the surface, for example; the scissors make little points all over the surface for a "porcupine" loaf.

Milk loaves can be very successfully baked under the tin, provided the right amount of dough is used to just fill the tin in the oven without tipping it over. This is a bit of an art, but once mastered the loaves are very pleasing to look at.

All milk loaves look nicer and have a softer crust if washed over with milk just as they come from the oven.

A further word about this sponge and dough method. The same method can with some advantage be used for ordinary white bread. The water is taken with an equal amount of flour (usually 10 oz from 1 lb), the yeast and any sugar. The remainder of the ingredients come on at the doughing up stage.

However, for some kinds of bread the softening of the gluten is more important than it is for milk bread, and so a different form of sponge is used, much stiffer and fermenting over more time.

Just before going on to that let me pass on how to increase the fermenting time of this sponge we have just been talking about without proving it for any longer. For this will improve the flavour still more if you have the time to wait for the sponge.

All you do is cut the yeast in the sponge from 1 oz to ½ oz and leave the sponge at 80°F for 2 *hours*, then mix the other ½ oz yeast into the second lot of milk. No more work, but you are responsible for looking after it for longer. Even better milk loaves. . . .

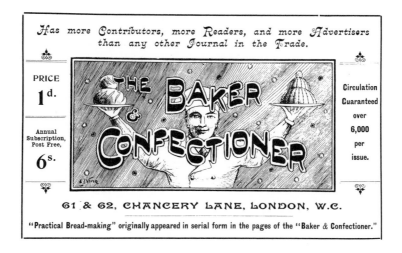

Coburgs and Cottages

Coburgs and cottages, fancy bricks and many other old-fashioned crusty loaves used to be baked on the firebrick sole of the oven. This makes a considerable difference to the crust both in texture and flavour and I have often been asked whether it is possible to reproduce anything like it in a modern domestic oven. The short answer is yes; but let us first consider what makes this nutty-crisp crust.

The bottom crust forms as soon as the bread goes into the oven. (With tin bread the bottom crust forms much more gradually.) The best way to get this is to acquire a thin fire-clay tile about one-foot square, which can be placed in the oven on a tray a few inches from the bottom. Then allow the tile to get fully hot before setting the proved loaf on it by hand. Finding such a tile will not be easy, and a good substitute is an oven tray: allow it to get hot first, then take it from the oven and set the proved loaf upon it, returning it straight away to the oven.

The remainder of the crust achieves its crispness from the steam in the oven during the early part of baking. A steady, even heat is necessary, and the steam must not be allowed to escape, especially during the first 15 minutes. This can best be done by covering the loaf, as soon as it is placed on the hot tray, with a round tin 10–12 inches in diameter and about 8 inches deep. Inside this the loaf will bake in an "oven" inside the oven. The "bonnet" (as this tin is called) should be big enough to cover a large loaf without any danger of touching. With a tray and such a bonnet, crusty bread at home becomes a distinct possibility.

Because this baking is so different from that used for tin breads, a different flavour is obtained. The sudden heating of the loaf can lead to all sorts of misshaping unless the fermentation and proof are correct and under proper control. The gluten needs to be pliable enough to move with this sudden expansion, but not so soft as to cause the bread to run out flat.

Good crusty loaves can be made on the straight dough process, or with a sponge and dough of the type used for making milk bread. However, there are easier ways of getting the right development, mainly through using a stiffer and longer sponge.

Sour dough

One thing that can help all bread, of whatever type, provided you are making it at least twice each week, is to place 2 oz of the current dough in a sealed polythene container (after thoroughly washing it, of course) and adding this to the next dough. Then wash the container in really hot water and put in 2 oz from the next dough. After a few shots at this, the little bit of dough becomes distinctly sour and very much like soft putty. It helps the next dough to mature, and adds wonderful homely flavour too. So make a habit of keeping 2 oz sour dough *in a cool place* all the time. It is not, however, a good idea to keep it longer than a week. This sour dough will improve all bread, but particularly crusty loaves, where good shape means such a lot.

Besides this, a long, stiff sponge will give part of the dough plenty of time to mature. And, finally, the kneading action will have to be more thorough than for anything else you make if these three components are to be smoothly mixed and the dough well made.

This is a real challenge if ever there was one. Anyone who can make a healthy, shapely Coburg or cottage loaf has a proven mastery of the art of breadmaking.

The loaves can be made with or without the sour dough, but it is included in the recipe so that it can be put in as soon as you have some. Doughs for oven-bottom bread need to be stiffer than usual, so be sure it is not made too soft; and note that the "sponge" described here is in fact a dough completely made and fermented, which is later worked well through more dough ingredients. Note also that the sponge is made cold and kept in a cool place: we don't want it to rise too quickly. The idea is that it can be made in the evening to ferment very slowly over-night for bread to be made the next day.

Coburg Bread — overnight sponge and dough

Sponge	8 oz	flour	230 g
	¼ oz	salt	7 g
	¼ oz	yeast	7 g
	4 oz	water	120 g

Take the water straight from the cold tap. With the flour, salt, yeast and water make a small, stiff dough. Place in a clean bowl or polythene container and cover with a damp cloth (try to ensure the cloth remains just a bit damp). Note that all the salt is in this sponge, to steady the yeast action, and also that the sponge is very stiff. As long as it is fully mixed there is no need to work it quite as much as an ordinary dough, because it will smooth out somewhat during the long standing. It should be put in a cool, draught-free place, and can be made up into dough at any time between 10 and 18 hours. Before taking it for doughing-up, it is as well not to touch it.

Dough	8 oz	flour	230 g
	½ oz	sugar	15 g
	½ oz	lard	15 g
	¾ oz	yeast	23 g
	6 oz	water	170 g
	2 oz	sour dough optional	60 g

Take the water at the correct temperature for 80°F dough +8°F. Break the sugar and yeast through the water. Rub the fat through the flour. Mix this dough just until all the flour is damped, but no more at this stage. Cut up the sponge into little bits and shake it through the mass (along with the sour dough, if used). Adjust the water content if necessary for a stiff dough, and then knead it hard until your arms are fit to drop off. Cover the dough with a damp cloth for 10 minutes only so that you and it can recover, then proceed to give it another good kneading before shaping it up nice and round, with a smooth surface like a baby's bottom.

Scatter some ground rice on the table and lay the top of the loaf on top. Fill the bonnet with water, turn it upside down to empty, then place it over the top of the loaf as a "prover".

When fully proved, carefully with a razor blade make two cuts about ¼ inch deep, to form a cross. The cuts should start and finish at the table.

Dust the hot tray with ground rice and very carefully place the loaf on it in the middle. Cover with the bonnet and place in a hot oven (500°F). Close the oven door and leave alone for half an hour.

At the half-hour, pull out the tray and lift the bonnet just to make sure that the baking is even. If not, turn the tray round but *don't move the loaf*. If you are confident that your oven gives even heat it is better to leave the bread alone. It will take 40 minutes or so to bake.

After taking it out, place it on the cooling wire and leave it to cool for an hour before slicing.

Your record sheet will help particularly with this kind of bread because the chances of getting perfect shape at the first shot are remote; but bit by bit the shape can be improved. The flavour and keeping of bread made in this way is so good that once you have tasted it you will very likely want to make even the tin bread in this way. This is possible, provided the kneading is thorough. Just remember that a tin loaf needs a slightly softer dough.

The cross on top of the loaf is said to originate with English housewives who put the sacred mark on so that the loaf would not be bewitched and turn out heavy. Certainly, the cuts release gases during "oven spring", which helps to improve the shape of the loaf and make it less solid.

The same recipe is used for all the British crusty loaves. Only the moulding shape and the cutting style differs. The shape must be suitable for fitting under the bonnet when the loaf is fully risen without touching it, but a square tin may help if you want a long loaf. Simply mould the bread as with a tin loaf and make about ten diagonal cuts with the blade just before setting it in the oven and you have a bloomer loaf. By making one cut about ½ inch deep along the full length of the centre of the loaf you have a split batten. The cutting helps to allow the loaf to expand naturally in the oven without bursting the crust.

The same dough can be used for making a **Cottage Loaf**. This is the most difficult of all loaves to make well, and has become something of a symbol of a good baker. Cottage loaves are not so often seen in shops nowadays because they take considerable skill to make well, especially every day in commercial batches.

Take about one-third of the dough for the top of the loaf, the rest for the bottom, and shape both pieces on the surface. Place the smaller piece on top. Cover with the bonnet and allow 5 minutes to recover before "bashing". Then bring the first two fingers of each hand together back-to-back and push them down through the centre of the loaf right through to the table. Seal the top and bottom pieces well with the fingers before removing them. Then leave the loaf to complete proving under the bonnet, and bake as with the Coburgs. Just before setting them in the oven they can be cut round the edges of top and bottom, cutting an upwards nick of about an inch in length every 2 or 3 inches all round. This gives the loaf "exhaust" outlets and helps to prevent it tipping over. Other kinds of fancy cuts can be used on the sides to make decorative patterns, but do remember that it should not take long to get the bread from the table into the oven.

Crusty breads from brown flours can be made in the same way, though they are never as successful as the white made by this method. It is far better to use a two-hour tin-bread dough and make it up a bit stiffer, although the use of a brown bread flour will help the shape.

Buns and Bun Loaves

These are made from a rich, soft dough and usually contain fruit. All bun goods need to be worked through warm (at 80°F) and in a moist environment. They are normally made on a "ferment and dough" process, which is similar to a very thin sponge that ferments vigorously for a very short time (about 10 minutes) just to get the yeast busy before tackling the harder job of lifting all that stodgy sugar and fat.

The fruit should always be picked over for stalks and stones, then washed and allowed to dry off a bit, either on a dry tea-towel or in a sieve. Wash the fruit just before use, to let it take in water and be nice and moist. However, because it is so soft and fleshy it must be added after the kneading of the dough, and mixed in carefully so that it does not burst and give unpleasant brown streaks in the dough. The fruit should also of course be warmed before it is added to the dough.

Bun loaves, like most varieties of buns, have a sticky, shiny top. This is because, immediately after baking, the tops are brushed over with bunwash, a syrup made by just bringing to the boil 5 oz sugar, 3 oz water and a squeeze of lemon juice.

Bun Loaves

Ferment			
10 oz	milk	280 g
¼ oz	sugar	7 g
2 oz	flour	60 g
1 oz	yeast	30 g

Warm the milk to 110°F and pour it into a bowl; mix in the sugar and then the yeast. Finally, whisk in the flour, cover with a damp cloth and leave to ferment for 10–15 minutes. During this time prepare the dough ingredients.

Dough			
14 oz	flour	400 g
¼ oz	salt	7 g
2 oz	fat	60 g
2 oz	sugar	60 g
2 oz	egg	60 g
	a pinch of cinnamon	

Mix the sugar and egg together (2 oz egg usually means one whole egg, unless it is unduly large or small). Leave this liquid on one side in a cup. Rub the salt, fat and cinnamon into the flour and make a bay.

When the ferment is ready, pour the egg and sugar into it and mix it thoroughly. Then pour the liquid into the bay and dough-up as usual. The dough should be quite soft but not sloppy; it must be possible to handle it — since we don't want to have to use too much dusting flour — although handling soft dough comes with experience.

This dough needs half an hour before the fruit is added, so keep it warm and covered meanwhile. Warm the fruit and mix it in gently but thoroughly so that it is evenly distributed. This dough will take 4 oz of dried fruit, which can be any combination of currants, sultanas, raisins, cut mixed peel or *glacé* cherries cut to the same size as the currants. Then give the dough a further 15 minutes under the cloth before dividing it into loaves to place in two loaf tins, either round or long. Prove warm and bake at 430°F–440°F. After taking them out of the oven, brush them with bunwash.

Plain Bun Loaves can be made simply by leaving out the fruit. Cherry and Walnut Bread uses 3 oz cut cherries and 3 oz broken walnuts (all about the size of currants) in place of the fruit. Date and Walnut Bread is made similarly, and so on.

If you don't like the sticky top, try brushing the loaves with egg instead just *before* they go in the oven.

Do make sure this bread is properly baked before taking it out, otherwise it will collapse when removed from the tins.

The same dough can be used to make buns; it is a good idea to make half into buns and the other half into a bun loaf. The buns should be weighed off at 1½ oz and moulded round. Place them on a clean, warmed and lightly greased tray, spaced out so that they will not touch when rising. Prove well and bake at 430°F–440°F until ready (about 15 minutes), turning the tray if necessary when they are part-done, so as to get them all the same colour. When they come out, brush them with bunwash and cool them on wires.

It is best to weigh all buns, even if they are not necessarily going to a shop, because unless they are a uniform size their baking times will vary. Also, a tray of identical-looking buns gives a nicer impression than a set of assorted sizes.

For a different bun loaf, space eight of these buns evenly in a cake tin, or make a ring of them close up on a tray. Wash them with egg, after proving, and pour a sprinkling of sugar on top of each (but *not* on the tray, where it will burn), or use white icing made by mixing icing sugar and water, poured over each bun-round after baking, and throw on a few more bits of cherry. Alternatively, try adding a little chopped crystallized ginger in with the fruit for a sharpening of the flavour.

The fruit can be left out altogether until moulding the loaves, and then rolled in, as with a Swiss roll, so that the fruit forms a spiral in each slice. If you like this idea, try mixing 1 oz butter and 1 oz brown sugar through the fruit before rolling it in for even better swirl bun loaves. Just make sure this filling is completely sealed into the dough; if it gets on to the tins it will burn on and take quite some getting off.

Another handy filling for rolling in this way (as long as it is spread thinly on the dough) is mincemeat. Pin out the dough big enough to take the filling and roll up in several turns, and dampen the last edge with water to make sure that it sticks downs. Seal the ends with your fingers.

To make an **Almond Swirl Loaf**, spread in 4 oz marzipan softened with enough egg-white to make it possible to spread it. Eggwash the top after proof, and sprinkle a few ground almonds on the top. Dust with icing sugar after baking.

If the rolling is neatly done, try putting a single lengthways cut with a razor blade right across the top about half an inch deep, just before baking. This should be just deep enough for the filling to be exposed down the middle and give another interesting finish.

The buns could be slightly flattened just before you place them on the tray, and then turned over when half-cooked. If being done like this they are better eggwashed before baking and not bunwashed.

With experience, many other variations can be thought up based on these ideas. Several favourite traditional bun-dough varieties can also be made using this dough. They are usually served buttered for tea, instead of or as well as scones.

Chelsea Buns

The same technique used for making the swirl loaves mentioned above. Make and ferment the plain bun dough, then pin it out with a rolling-pin to a rectangle about 12 inches by 18 inches. Spread this with melted butter, over which is scattered 1 oz brown sugar mixed with ¼ oz cinnamon. Follow this by 4 oz currants and roll up the sheet tightly. Wash it with butter, then cut it into about sixteen equal slices, placing these flat on a warm greased tray, with the edges just touching, four buns across and four down. Eggwash and dust them with castor sugar. Prove the sheet until the pieces form squares by joining together, then bake at 420°F.

Swiss Buns can be made by using plain bun dough, scaled at 1½ oz after fermentation, moulded round and left covered on the table for 10 minutes. Then, carefully roll them to about 3 inches long and place on a warmed, lightly greased tray to prove. Make sure there is plenty of room between them so that they don't join together during proof. When proved, bake at 430°F–440°F, allow to cool, then ice the tops with a stiff mixture of warm water and icing sugar to which has been added the juice of half a lemon. The flavour can be helped if the other half of the lemon goes into the ferment in place of the same amount of milk.

Hot Cross Buns are made in just the same way as the fruit buns mentioned above, but with the addition of a few drops of bunspice to the egg used in the dough, and of course the cross motif on the top. Bunspice can be bought from a delicatessen shop or from an overworked baker. The crosses are piped on to the buns just before baking, with a plain tube of about ⅛ inch or through a hole of ⅛ inch in a paper bag. Make the paste by rubbing together 4 oz self-raising flour and 1 oz fat, then mix thoroughly with 4 oz milk, or enough to make a paste that can easily be piped in lines over the buns. Beat this well. It is easier to pipe on the crosses if you put the buns on the tray in straight lines. After baking, the buns should be bunwashed while still hot — and of course if they are really to live up to their name they ought to be eaten hot, too.

Cream Splits are made by moulding round 2 oz pieces of plain bun dough on to warmed trays, proving and baking at 450°F–460°F. When they have cooled, cut them almost in half. Put in a spot of raspberry jam and a good squirt of whipped fresh cream. Replace the tops lightly and dust over with icing sugar. Eat them on the same day.

Devon Chudleighs require a similar bun dough but with butter used in place of fat. When fermented, scale the dough at 2 oz and shape round. Place them close together on a clean, lightly greased tray, so that they all stick together and come out square with round tops. Prove and bake as usual, though they will take a little longer since they are joined together. After baking, they should be brushed with bunwash and allowed to cool. Serve them with whipped or clotted cream and home-made strawberry jam.

Saffron Buns are mainly made in Cornwall and have a distinctive flavour and colour from the saffron infusion in the dough (saffron is a member of the crocus family). Now that dried flowers are more readily available elsewhere, these lovely buns deserve to become more widely known.

First you need to make saffron tea, using ¼ oz (7 g) finely cut saffron to ½ pint (280 g) boiling water. Add 3 oz (85 g) granulated sugar and allow to stand for half an hour. Boil it again, then allow it to get almost cold before straining through fine muslin and bottling for use. Do not make in large quantities, for it does not keep well after two or three days.

Add to the bun dough at the rate of 1 oz per mix in place of 1 oz milk, but do not add it until the ferment is ready. Omit the cinnamon, although you could add a few drops of lemon juice. Weigh at 2 oz, mould round, allow 10 minutes to recover, then pin out to ½ inch thick; wash with milk and dip in castor sugar, before spacing out well on a clean, lightly greased tray. Prove and bake as for buns.

Almond Buns will require 4 oz (115 g) marzipan paste, 6 oz (180 g) castor sugar and enough egg to make a soft paste. This paste should be properly mixed so that there are no lumps or hard bits in it. Scale ordinary bun dough at 2 oz and shape each piece round. Leave on a floured table for 10 minutes upside down. Take roughly ½ inch pieces of the almond paste and shape them round. Flatten each bun and place almond paste in the middle. Fold the dough over envelope-fashion to form a square with the paste well sealed inside. Wash with diluted egg, keeping the folds down on the tray, and dredge with castor sugar. Nick each bun twice with the tip of a knife. Prove and bake in the normal way.

Helvetia Buns are a special treat to test the skills of enthusiastic bun-makers. You will need 8 oz (230 g) puff pastry, either self-prepared or the purchased frozen variety. The curd filling requires:

8 oz	cottage cheese	230 g
3 oz	butter	90 g
3 oz	sugar	90 g
3½ oz	egg	95 g
2 oz	currants	60 g
	a small pinch of nutmeg	

Cream the butter, nutmeg and sugar, then add the eggs a little at a time. Mix in the cottage cheese and finally the currants.

You also need bun dough, which should be pinned out about 20 inches square with a rolling-pin. Dampen the dough but don't wet it; this is easiest done by wringing out a clean, wet, tea-towel, opening it up and laying it over the dough for a moment, patting it lightly all over. Elsewhere on the table, pin out the puff pastry to the same size, then lay it over the dough and gently stick it down. Spread about half the curd on two-thirds of the pastry; fold the uncovered part over, then fold the curd right in, making three layers of dough, three of puff pastry and two of curd mixture. Press to remove any air-pockets, then cut into strips 2 inches by 3½ inches. Prove, and bake at 450°F. Afterwards, brush over with icing made by adding enough icing sugar to the juice of one lemon to achieve a manageable consistency.

The other half of the curd mixture could be used to make some more tomorrow — it keeps for four days in the fridge. It also makes a wonderful filling for tarts or pie-cases lined with plain pastry.

The Bath Bun and Sally Lunn of the Regency Period

These recipes have been tested and adapted from quite old sources. When I first came across them I was amazed to discover that neither were anything like the articles made today under the same names; it was like coming across something completely new and fine. Hard times may more than once have affected the availability of materials or of skill, knowledge and time. The traditional item has gradually been cheapened out of all recognition, to the point of almost becoming lost, as can easily happen when a name is retained by something that is no longer authentic. So let's try some old recipes.

Bath Buns

Ferment			
	5 oz	milk	140 g
	½ oz	sugar	14 g
	2 oz	flour	60 g
	¾ oz	yeast	20 g

Warm milk to 110°F and pour it into a bowl. Mix the milk with sugar, then the yeast. Finally, whisk the flour in vigorously and leave to ferment for 20 minutes in a warm place (not hot, please).

Dough	1 lb 0 oz	strong flour	460 g
	8 oz	butter	230 g
	6 oz	eggs	175 g
	1 oz	yolk	30 g
		grated zest of ½ lemon	
		a pinch of grated nutmeg	

Mix the sugar, egg and yolk together. Leave this liquid to one side in a cup. Next, rub the butter, nutmeg and lemon zest into the flour and make a bay.

When the ferment is ready, pour the eggs, yolk and sugar into it, then pour it into the bay and dough up in the usual way. The dough must be quite soft and should be very well worked. Place the dough in a warm place with a damp cloth over it to prevent chilling or skinning. It needs to ferment for an hour. Then knock it back well, and replace for a further half-hour.

After the dough is ready

9 oz	coarse sugar nibs	250 g
3 oz	finely shredded citron peel	85 g
2 oz	finely shredded orange peel	55 g

The citron and orange peel can be replaced by mixed peel if that is all that is available. I prefer to chop it very fine with a cook's knife rather than waste some of the peel in a mincer and have the extra chore of cleaning it out. But minced peel will do; you want the flavours, not the tough little cubes. Do not, however, go to the other extreme and pulp it!

Lay the dough pieces out roughly on clean, lightly greased trays, so they are rocky on top, but all the same size and shape. This quantity will make thirty buns, which should not be set too closely together. Eggwash them, then dust with sugar nibs. Prove carefully in the open (i.e. uncovered). When they have doubled their size, bake them to a rich bright colour at 380°F (193°F). Cool them on wires before eating — if you can wait!

Sally Lunns

10 oz	milk	280 g
¼ oz	honey	7 g
2 oz	flour	60 g
1 oz	salt	30 g

Warm the milk to 110°F and pour into a bowl. Mix in the honey, then the yeast and finally the flour. Cover with a damp cloth and leave to ferment for 15 minutes. During this time prepare the following dough ingredients.

Dough	1 lb 0 oz	strong flour	460 g
	2½ oz	butter	90 g
	2½ oz	sugar	90 g
	2 oz	egg	60 g
		grated zest of ½ lemon	
		a little grated nutmeg	
		a pinch of salt	

Sieve the flour on to the table, then rub in the butter; make a bay, into which break the eggs, put in the lemon and nutmeg. Dissolve the sugar in the ferment, pour into the bay, then mix to a smooth dough, kneading thoroughly.

Ferment in a warm place for one hour. Knock back, allow half an hour for recovery, then weigh at 6 oz and mould the pieces round on to the table. Allow 10 minutes' recovery under a cloth to prevent skimming. Remould and drop into warmed 4-inch cake hoops which have been lined with greaseproof paper. Press a hole in the centre of each, then prove until they are 2 inches above the top of the tins, before baking carefully at 400°F. Then brush over with a mixture of:

10 oz	milk	280 g
2 oz	egg	60 g
1 oz	sugar	30 g

I understand that Sally Lunns used to be served hot for breakfast, but that depended on someone getting up pretty early to start making them! Teatime is better. Split them open while they are hot and serve them with whipped cream — and strawberries or raspberries when in season.

Victorian Bun Rounds

Another English classic is the bun round — originally highly distinctive and well worth bringing back.

Bun Rounds

Ferment	10 oz	milk	280 g
	¼ oz	sugar	7 g
	2 oz	flour	55 g
	1 oz	yeast	28 g

Warm the milk to 110°F and pour it into a bowl, then mix in the sugar, followed by the yeast. Finally, whisk in the flour, cover with a damp cloth and leave for 10–15 minutes. During this time, prepare the dough.

Dough	1 lb 0 oz	bread flour	460 g
	1½ oz	sugar	40 g
	⅛ oz	salt	5 g
	2 oz	butter	55 g
	2 oz	eggs	55 g

Dissolve the sugar into the eggs and mix in the ferment. Rub the butter and salt into the flour and make a bay on the table. Pour the ferment into this and dough up as usual. The dough should be quite soft but not sticky; if it is made too soft it will be impossible to handle.

Scale the dough at 3 oz and split into two. Mould the pieces round and allow them to recover. Roll them out at 3½-inch diameter and eggwash the edges. Place a little mincemeat (about 1 oz) in the centre of each, then fold the dough over three times to form a triangle. Place seven of these on a clean, lightly greased tray to form a heptagon. Eggwash and drop a little sugar over the join of each piece. Prove, then bake at 420°F, afterwards cooling on wires.

Dough Cakes and Fermented Cakes

Before the invention of baking powder, many more cakes were made from fermented dough. Nowadays they are rarely seen, although they all have a quality of their own which it would be well worth bringing back. Most of the recipes are on the borderline between fermented goods (breads) and confectionery (cakes).

Wiesbaden Buncakes

Sponge	10 oz	milk at 95°F	280 g
	1 oz	yeast	30 g
	8 oz	flour	230 g

Whisk the yeast into the milk, then mix in the flour and beat well. Scrape down. Allow to ferment for half an hour while you prepare clean, well greased savarin rings or sandwich-cake tins. Sprinkle a few flaked almonds, hazelnuts or peanuts into these prepared tins.

Batter			
	6 oz	butter	170 g
	3 oz	sugar	85 g
	6 oz	eggs	170 g
	5 oz	currants	145 g
	2 oz	sultanas	60 g
	1 oz	chopped peel	30 g

Cream up the butter and sugar, add the eggs over four stages, beating and scraping down between each addition. The eggs and batter alike should be at about 70°F. When all the eggs are in, mix the flour in and, finally, gently but completely mix in the yeast sponge mixture. Put the batter in the tins to about two-thirds full. Prove for about half an hour, then bake at about 400°F. Cool on wires, before icing with thin water icing.

Old-fashioned Dough Cakes

For each of these a common dough is made, using for the ferment:

10 oz	milk at 110°F	280 g
¼ oz	sugar	7 g
2 oz	flour	60 g
1 oz	yeast	30 g

Make up as for buns, and ferment for 15 minutes. Then dough up with:

14 oz	flour	400 g
¼ oz	salt	7 g
1 oz	lard	30 g

Country Dough Cake

1 lb 8 oz	dough	690 g
4½ oz	butter	130 g
4½ oz	sugar	130 g
12 oz	mixed fruit	340 g

¼ oz	ground nutmeg	7 g
½ oz	lemon juice and zest	15 g

Thoroughly mix all the ingredients together, then divide into greased cake or bread tins. Prove, then bake at 420°F.

Another Dough Cake

1 lb 8 oz	dough	690 g
6 oz	butter	170 g
4½ oz	sugar	130 g
4½ oz	eggs	130 g
¼ oz	nutmeg and cinnamon	7 g
1 lb 2 oz	mixed fruits	510 g

Thoroughly mix all the ingredients together, then divide into greased cake or bread tins. Prove, then bake at 420°F.

Yet another dough cake recipe again uses 1½ lb dough but with 3 oz (85 g) lard, 3 oz (85 g) brown sugar, 9 oz (260 g) mixed fruits and a choice of spices. Proceed as for the other dough cakes. Brown or white sugar are interchangeable, and brown flour can be used instead of white, although the cakes may be a bit dry and solid if you don't use at least a proportion of strong white flour.

From these variations you will be able to create your own.

Fermented Cake

Ferment			
	10 oz	milk at 100°F	280 g
	¼ oz	sugar or honey	7 g
	2 oz	flour	60 g
	1 oz	yeast	30 g

Make up this ferment and leave it in a warm place.

Batter			
	1 lb 0 oz	flour	460 g
	3½ oz	sugar	100 g
	8 oz	butter	230 g
	8 oz	eggs	230 g
	2 lb 4 oz	mixed fruit	1020 g

1 lb 14 oz	milk	850 g
¼ oz	mixed spice	7 g
½ oz	lemon zest	15 g

Cream the butter, flavours and sugar. Add the eggs gradually, then the flour, ferment and remainder of the milk. Scrape down and mix in the fruit. Divide into well-greased tins, two-thirds filling each. Prove for half an hour in a warm place before baking steadily at 400°F.

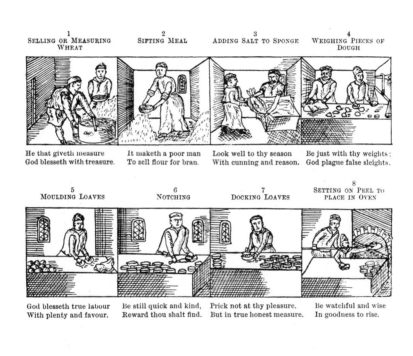

<table>
<tr><td>1
SELLING OR MEASURING
WHEAT</td><td>2
SIFTING MEAL</td><td>3
ADDING SALT TO SPONGE</td><td>4
WEIGHING PIECES OF
DOUGH</td></tr>
<tr><td>He that giveth measure
God blesseth with treasure.</td><td>It maketh a poor man
To sell flour for bran.</td><td>Look well to thy season
With cunning and reason.</td><td>Be just with thy weights;
God plague false sleights.</td></tr>
</table>

<table>
<tr><td>5
MOULDING LOAVES</td><td>6
NOTCHING</td><td>7
DOCKING LOAVES</td><td>8
SETTING ON PEEL TO
PLACE IN OVEN</td></tr>
<tr><td>God blesseth true labour
With plenty and favour.</td><td>Be still quick and kind,
Reward thou shalt find.</td><td>Prick not at thy pleasure,
But in true honest measure.</td><td>Be watchful and wise
In goodness to rise.</td></tr>
</table>

THE MYSTERIE AND TRADE OF BAKING

All services that to the Baker's Trade
Or mysterie belong, be here displaid,

Which my rude Arts in order shall recount,
And those in number to thirteen amount,
Being (how ere such Tradesmen used to coozen
In their scale measure) just a Baker's dozen.

First [1] Boulting, [2] Seasoning, [3] Casting up, and [4] Braking,
[5] Breaking out dowe, next [6] Weighing, or weight making
(Which last is rarely seene), then some doe [7] Mould;
This [8] Cuts, that [9] Seales and Sets up, yet behold

The seasoner [10] Heating, or with Barin fires
Preparing the oven as the case requires;
One carrying up, the Heeter peeleth on
And playes the [11] Setter, who's no sooner gone

But the hot mouth is [12] Stopt, so to remaine
Untill the setter [13] drawes all forth againe.

Thus bakers make and to perfection bring,
No less to serve the Beggar than the King,
All sorts of Bread, which being handled well,
All other food and Cates doth farre excell.

Let Butchers, Poultrers, Fishmongers contend
Each in his own trade, in what he can Defend,
Though Flesh, Fish, Whitemeat, all in fitting season,
Nourish the body, being used with reason,

Yet no man can deny (to end the strife)
Bread is worth all, being the staff of life.

Barm Bracks and Lardy Cakes

It is worth mentioning again that a good deal of the "old-fashioned" flavour resulted from the fact that people didn't use yeast as we know it, but either drew their own from the bottom of the home-brewed ale (a very tasty source) or bought it in liquid form from the local brewery. It was probably this which led to the many country recipes for beer cake when the old fermented flavour was disappearing from fruit cake. Of course, another way of keeping fermented flavours in fruit cake was with the addition before and/or after baking of spirits, especially brandy and rum. But this activity, however attractive, was a bit like cheating to those who had grown up with the natural fermentation flavours as familiar as those of home-made cheese, ale and bread.

Beer cake may not be quite the same as a barm cake made over three days, but it carries the same nostalgic flavour to some degree.

Beer Fruit Cake

1 lb 0 oz	plain flour	460 g
6 oz	butter	180 g
6 oz	brown sugar	180 g
6 oz	currants	180 g
1 oz	mixed peel	30 g
4 oz	eggs	120 g
10 oz	beer (½ pint)	300 g
½ oz	baking powder	15 g

Grease two loaf tins well and set the oven at 350°F. Cream the butter and sugar. Add the currants, peel, flour and baking powder. Beat the eggs with the beer, then add to the mixture and mix well. Divide into the two tins and bake in the centre of the oven for about an hour.

Barm Brack

A heavily fruited loaf, very popular in Ireland, the barm brack was originally made using liquor in which yeast was grown. The long fermentation plays an important part in the development of its flavour.

Sponge	10 oz	milk	300 g
	½ oz	honey	15 g
	¼ oz	yeast	7 g
	10 oz	flour	300 g
	2 oz	egg (1 egg)	60 g
	very small pinch of cinnamon and nutmeg		

Warm the milk to 110°F. Pour it into a bowl and mix in the honey, then the yeast. Finally beat in the flour. Cover with a damp cloth and ferment for 5–6 hours. It it is more convenient, you could halve the yeast quantity and ferment it for twice as long, since it is here that you get the flavour.

Next, add ¾ oz yeast dispersed in a little water, and then one egg. Beat in and scrape the mixture down before adding the following to make the dough:

Dough	6 oz	flour	180 g
	¼ oz	salt	7 g
	2 oz	butter	60 g
	1½ oz	honey	45 g

Make into a very soft dough and mix well. Allow to stand for half an hour, before adding fruit as follows:

Fruit			
	8 oz	sultanas	240 g
	8 oz	currants	240 g
	2 oz	cherries	60 g
	2 oz	chopped peel	60 g

When mixed, scale off at 1 lb (480 g) and shape round. Place in clean, greased loaf tins and prove until they have doubled in size. Wash with egg, then bake at 380°F (190°C). Make sure they are fully baked. They will take about an hour. Cool them on wires, then wrap in foil and keep for about three days. When taken out and sliced they have the most wonderful smell. Butter them and serve with cream cheese for a really pleasurable experience.

Oxford Lardy Cakes

(a)			
	1 lb 0 oz	strong flour	460 g
	¼ oz	salt	7 g
	8 oz	lard	230 g
	½ oz	yeast	15 g
	9–10 oz	milk	270–300 g
(b)	6 oz	lard	180 g
	3 oz	brown sugar	90 g
		a little spice	

Make a dough with (a), at 80°F, and allow it to ferment for 1 hour. Mix (b) together. You can use mixed spices or blend your own. Favourites would include ground ginger, cinnamon and nutmeg, and you can add a squeeze of lemon juice as well if desired.

Pin the dough (a) out to a rectangle. Cover two-thirds of it with part of the filling (b); fold half the dough over the filling used, then fold the other half over, so that the filling is enclosed. Pin out again and fold into three after spreading the remainder of the filling inside.

Cut into two pieces and place in rectangular tins about 8 inches × 6 inches. Brush the top with a mixture of milk and egg, and score a trellis design on the top with a knife. Allow to prove before baking at 420°F.

Gloucester Lardy Cakes

This is my own favourite — wonderful for families in the winter.
  To the Oxford Lardy Cake dough (a), add:

6 oz	sultanas	180 g
2 oz	currants	60 g

Pin out this dough. Make a filling mixture with:

6 oz	lard	180 g
6 oz	brown sugar	180 g
⅛ oz	ground spice	3 g

Spread the filling over the dough, then fold into three. Pin out again and fold into three. Then pin out to a rectangle and roll out like a fat Swiss roll. Cut into three and place each circle in a greased round cake tin. Bake at 420°F. Turn them upside down on to cloths or wires immediately on taking them from the oven, otherwise they will stick. The brown sugar and lard sets on cooling to form a lovely glaze.

Wiltshire Lardy Cake

Again use the Oxford Lardy Cake (a) dough, with the addition of 4 oz currants. Ferment for 1 hour. Pin out, and spread on the following mixture:

12 oz	lard	180 g
3 oz	castor sugar	90 g
⅛ oz	mixed spice	3 g

Fold three times, pin out, fold three times, then pin out to about 16 inches × 12 inches and place on a tray. Eggwash and mark the top with a knife. Prove, then bake at 420°F. When cool, cut into slices or square 3 inches × 1½ inches or 2 inches × 2 inches.

Teacakes and Scottish Baps

Born, reared and apprenticed to the baking trade in Yorkshire, I used to take Yorkshire teacakes very much for granted. Every baker made them in large quantities in the early hours of every morning, as they were regarded as a vital part of the daily diet of nearly everyone in the north of England. Each area has its own particular favourite kind of bread, which is made in a somewhat special way to suit local tastes. When I worked for several years away from Yorkshire the teacakes were among the things I missed most.

Yorkshire teacakes were originally made to contain a complete meal which the woollen workers could take into the mill with them. Teacakes do not dry up as slices of bread do when made into sandwiches. After cooling, the teacakes were rolled in a cloth and put in a bread crock (a large earthenware pot), where they were reputed to keep for a week or ten days and still be delicious toasted.

They are made in three main varieties: plain, fruited and wholemeal. The plain ones contain less sugar because they are often filled with ham or other savoury fillings. The older recipes recommend a little nutmeg in the fruited variety, which are usually fruited with currants alone.

The mixture should be white, in other words containing no eggs or colouring. Many people prefer a ferment and dough process, but if the yeast is good there is little to be gained by taking the extra trouble. The dough must be kept warm (80°F) throughout and not allowed to skin over; it should be soft and silky, full of life. For this, a fairly short process is preferable, with great care being taken over fermentation and proving times and temperatures.

The same recipe can be adapted for other kinds of teacakes which use the dough in a slightly different way.

Plain Teacakes

1 lb 0 oz	flour	460 g
¼ oz	salt	7 g
½ oz	sugar	15 g
10 oz	milk (approx.)	300 g
2 oz	lard	60 g
1 oz	yeast	30 g

Straight dough method at 80°F. Bulk fermentation time 1 hour. Knock back after 40 minutes. When ready, weigh off into seven teacakes of 4 oz each. Mould them round and place, moulding crease down, on a lightly floured table or board, spaced out so they will not stick while rising. Cover and allow 10 minutes to recover. When laying them on the board, put them down in an order you can remember, so that they can be taken up in the same order and thus get equal recovery.

During this 10 minute period warm, clean and lightly grease enough flat trays for the teacakes. The trays should be neither hot nor cold, but just warm enough to keep the dough at 80°F.

Pin out the teacakes (using as little flour as possible for dusting) to 4 inches – 4½ inches (10 cms) round; this is most easily done by pinning out one or two at a time, once north and once south, then turn them to east and west and repeat. Place them on the trays with at least 2 inches between each, and between them and the edge of the tray. Prove warm and moist, and when they are nicely plump bake them to a light golden brown at 480°F. After they come out, cool them on a wire and pack base to base.

For **Yorkshire Teacakes**, they must not be decorated in any way before baking and must not be washed over. They should have a velvety colour on top, fading to almost white down the sides. They should be perfectly round and about 1 inch thick, and when baked if nipped between finger and thumb they should spring back to full plumpness again.

If you get a large hole just under the top crust (a common fault at first), this means that the fermentation was incorrect, they were put in the oven too soon, or too much pressure was used during pinning.

Durham Teacakes are almost exactly the same except a bit thicker. Do not pin them out so much. **London Teacakes** are made in the south of England, weighed off at half the weight of their northern cousins, pricked in the middle three or four times with a fork, washed with egg when placed on the tray, and turned over when half-baked. Either of these varieties can also be made fruited or brown.

Currant Teacakes

1 lb 0 oz	flour	460 g	
¼ oz	salt	7 g	
2 oz	sugar	60 g	
2 oz	fat	60 g	
10 oz	milk (approx.)	300 g	
1 oz	yeast	30 g	
4 oz	currants	120 g	

Straight dough method at 80°F. Leave out the currants until knock-back stage at 40 minutes. Add fruit washed, dried and warm, gently mixing it thoroughly until evenly distributed throughout the dough. Ferment for a further 20 minutes, then proceed as for Plain Teacakes, but except that the yield is eight cakes of 4 oz, and because of the extra sugar the baking temperature needs to be brought down to 450°F–460°F.

Brown Teacakes

13 oz	wholemeal	390 g	
3 oz	flour	70 g	
¼ oz	salt	7 g	
½ oz	treacle	15 g	
10 oz	milk (approx.)	300 g	
2 oz	lard	60 g	
1 oz	yeast	30 g	

Straight dough method at 80°F. Details for working exactly as for Plain Teacakes.

It is usual to split and butter the teacakes, and with the plain or wholemeal ones use any sandwich filling. They are, however, very suitable for serving split, buttered and open as a base for a knife-and-fork open sandwich with cold meat or fish and salad items, or fried on the inside and used as a base for hot breakfasts of bacon, eggs, sausages, kidneys and so on. For afternoon tea they are more often sliced and buttered and served with preserves. When a few days old they toast extremely well: first toast whole top and bottom, then split them and toast the insides before buttering.

Some people confuse these teacakes with Scottish Baps, but in fact the two types of bread are not at all similar to eat. The Scottish Bap is a kind of roll made mainly for the breakfast table, and the method of making suggested below is designed to enable them to be made and on the table within just over an hour of getting out of bed — allowing time in between jobs to fry the usual eggs, ham, sausages and what have you to accompany them. What a way to live!

Obviously such speed can only be achieved using an overnight sponge and dough, but this will also help both the flavour and the lightness of the baps.

Scottish Baps

Overnight sponge and dough method. Note that the sponge is the same as that used for the Coburg dough (page 65), so if you are making Coburgs "tomorrow" just double up the sponge recipe and halve the sponge for the baps.

Sponge			
8 oz	flour	230 g
¼ oz	salt	7 g
¼ oz	yeast	7 g
4 oz	water	120 g

Take the water straight from the cold tap and make a stiff dough; ferment in a bowl under a damp cloth, in a cool but draught-free place for 10–18 hours. To save time, weigh up dough ingredients (except water) the night before.

Dough			
8 oz	flour	230 g
½ oz	sugar	15 g
1 oz	lard	30 g

6 oz	water	170 g
1 oz	yeast	30 g
1 oz	sour dough (optional)	30 g

Take the water at the correct temperature for an 80°F dough + 8°F. Make up the dough as directed for Coburg sponge and dough. Mix very thoroughly indeed. The dough should be softer than for the Coburgs and you may need to add more water for this. If it is not fairly soft you will not get the lift.

When thoroughly kneaded, put the dough in a warm bowl and cover with a damp cloth. Leave for 15 minutes only, then tear down well again and weight off at 3 oz pieces straight away. Mould them round, roll to about 2½ inches long and lay them on a floured table or board. After covering them for 10 minutes, pin them out, two at a time and not too thinly, this time lengthways, then lay them on clean, warmed and lightly greased trays, nicely spaced out. Prove warm, not too much, and then dust them thinly with flour on top and bake in a very hot oven (500°F). Be careful not to overbake them.

They are best eaten while fresh, and the overnight sponge will give them plenty of flavour.

Doughnuts

If you really want your digestive system to have a party, while greasing the insides of your children in preparation for a cold winter, then why not make scrumptious doughnuts?

The dough to use is the plain bun dough, just a little bit stiffer than for buns or bun loaves or else they will be difficult to lift into the pan when fully proved. When it is ready, scale the dough at 1½ oz each piece. If you can't manage the full mixing at one go, cut the dough in half and knock half of it down to rise again while working off the first half.

Doughnuts can be made into several shapes, although the **Doughnut Rings** are the most common. For these, each piece of dough is moulded round and pinned flat, the hole being cut out with a small cutter. (A small piece of piping from the plumber will do just as well if it is clean.) The "holes" can be collected up to make more doughnuts or dropped into the sour-dough container for use the next day.

Jam Doughnuts are usually moulded round. You can then just prove them and fry them, and put the jam in afterwards. But some enthusiasts, always on the lookout for ways of making life difficult, put a squirt of jam in the flattened doughnut before proving it, then fold the dough round it and seal it inside. If it is well sealed, and the doughnut properly proved and fried, there will be no trace in the finished article of how the jam got in. All very spectacular stuff really, but if the jam does find a way out during frying, the fat will be spoilt and so will the doughnuts. If you have a bit of mischief in you, try it by all means.

Don't, however, try doing it with **Cream Doughnuts**. These are rolled out boat shaped, and are the only doughnuts which are never rolled in cinnamon sugar after cooling. They should be almost split, spotted with a little raspberry jam, and then liberally filled with whipped cream. Obviously the cream must not be put in until they are cold. Replace the lid and dust them with icing sugar.

The pieces of dough in all cases are proved on warm greased trays, *not* in steam. A slight skinning is regarded as an advantage, provided it only appears towards the end of proof.

For frying, use either pure lard or frying oil. A deep pan is required, preferably a chip pan. All frying should be done at 370°F–380°F, and it is worthwhile using a thermometer to check this. If the fat is too hot the doughnuts will be dumpy and heavy. If it is too cool they will be heavy and fatty.

After frying, turning over at half-time, they should be cooled before rolling in an even mixture of 8 oz castor sugar and a pinch of cinnamon, although there are other kinds of finishes described below. If the doughnuts are rolled in sugar before the steam has cleared off them, the moisture of the doughnuts wets the sugar and spoils them, apart from wasting the sugar.

There are lots of other ways of finishing doughnuts, using different shapes and icing with water icing (as used on Swiss buns) with various colours and flavours. For example, try flavouring the icing with a spoonful of instant coffee, and filling with a stiffly made cornflour custard instead of cream.

Soft Rolls: Plain and Fancy

Good rolls provide one of the most delightful parts of a meal, and yet few restaurants of quality take half as much trouble over making and purchasing the right quality rolls as they do over the quality of their soups. It is unfortunate that so few people complain when offered a slice off a plant loaf, or one of those all-too-common huge, stodgy, flaky-crusted football rolls.

A good dinner roll has a very thin crisp crust that can only be made by using a special oven, into which steam is injected during the early part of baking. This type of oven is known as a Vienna oven and the crusty bread baked in it is Vienna bread; true dinner rolls are cooked in this way and so are Vienna rolls.

Any kind of imitation of this method of baking must leave something to be desired, so Vienna baking is really something that the kitchen connoisseur should leave to the professionals. Good Vienna rolls *can* be bought, though they may take some shopping for. When you find a baker who sells them, to ensure that you get them fresh for your own dinner party, ask when they are made and place an order in advance for a dozen. It may be worthwhile fixing your dinner to fit in with his roll-baking where possible. If your baker does not have a Vienna oven and someone who knows how to use it, your own rolls will probably be better anyway. Alternatively, serve Crissinii.

The rolls used for breakfast and tea, however, are usually soft-crusted, although a crisp roll is common with breakfast in continental Europe. A breakfast roll should be plain and not too rich. The dough used for Scottish Baps is ideal, since of course these are a form of breakfast roll.

Breakfast Rolls

1 lb 0 oz	flour	460 g
¼ oz	salt	7 g
10 oz	water and milk	280 g
1 oz	lard	30 g
1 oz	yeast	30 g
(+ 1 oz	sour dough optional)	30 g

Use about half water and half milk. Straight dough method at 80°F. To get the desirable uneven soft texture, try just gently folding over the dough a couple of times every quarter of an hour for 1 hour, instead of the more usual battle at knock-back. This holey texture is delightful to butter fresh at breakfast, so try to get all the kneading done at the dough-making stage.

Scale off when ready at 1½ oz each roll and shape them round or boat-shape. Place directly on warmed, clean, lightly greased trays. Prove nicely and bake at 480°F–500°F. Wash the tops with milk as soon as the rolls come out of the oven.

If they are made the day before use, just pop them back in the oven at about 350°F for a few minutes to freshen up while breakfast is being prepared. Stale rolls are a bad start to the day.

There are those who feel that breakfast, especially if it is as popular and varied as mine, ought to include pretty well the day's supply of inner cleanliness, and there may well be something in this. But purchased prep-arations are often costly and never freshly made. Breakfast cereals make beneficial use of the whole of the wheat, and especially the bran which has been mentioned. But all these benefits can be added to that of freshness for less money by making your own wholemeal breakfast rolls.

Health Breakfast Rolls

The word "health" is used here only because many people have come to equate health with lashings of indigestible bran. Some roughage is probably called for to balance other breakfast foods like kippers, trout, ham, eggs, kidneys and so on. But the word itself is no more valid than the word "sunshine" which indicates that the sun shone some of the time while the grain was ripening.

1 lb 0 oz	wholemeal	460 g
¼ oz	salt	7 g
10 oz	water and milk	280 g
1 oz	lard or butter	30 g
½ oz	honey or malt extract	15 g
1 oz	yeast	30 g

The rolls are made up exactly as the breakfast rolls except they are washed with milk before setting them on the tray, and the tops dipped in wholemeal flour. Better still, dip them in bran if you can buy some. Then sprinkle a very light dusting of salt on top of that just so that the bran is also salted and therefore tasty. Prove well. There is no need to fear skinning because of the washing with milk etc., but keep them warm. When proved, make a small cut on the top of each for decoration and to let surplus gas out, and bake them at 480°F–500°F.

Now there are several things you can do with these rolls besides just eat them at breakfast. Any left over should be sliced thinly with a sharp ham knife, preferably when a day old. They should be cut as thinly as possible without crumbing them too much. Then dip the slices in a mixture of 3 oz milk and 1 oz honey or malt extract, and lay them on a baking tray to dry for an hour or so. Then bake them off in a cool oven (300°F–350°F) until thoroughly dry. If they are well dried they will keep in a polythene tub almost indefinitely. Try them as your own make of breakfast cereal.

If you have difficulty dipping the slices, try dabbing the milk and honey on top with a brush. Or cut the slices thicker and make ¼ inch cubes to dip in. Or break it right down into crumbs and mix enough honey, milk and egg white to make a paste; then spread the paste on a tray covered with a well-greased sheet of greaseproof paper, dry it all out in the oven then peel off the paper and store the flakes.

Once you start experimenting with your own cereals you will find that this kind of idea lends itself to many variations. But, of course, none of them have much to do with the soft rolls this is supposed to be about. . . .

Tea rolls are a different business altogether. They are actually the same as bridge rolls and belong with teacakes, scones and bun goods on the tea table. The recipe includes egg, but only an ounce in our standard-size mix. Bridge or tea rolls are small and dainty, so the recipe makes what may seem rather a lot. They do, however, have a tendency to disappear rather quickly.

A half-size dough can be made, and this is better if the oven will not take the full quantity. But with a dough so small it is not easy to keep control over the fermentation and the possibility of skinning, so do take great care.

Bridge rolls are shaped long like small frankfurter sausages. To achieve this they are first moulded round, then rolled long. It takes some practice to get them the same width throughout the length of the roll and have them all exactly the same shape and size. But it is worth it, for then the set will not only look nicer, they will also fill more easily. The flour used may be white, or for brown rolls just use the same recipe but with whole-meal flour instead of white.

Bridge Rolls

1 lb 0 oz	flour		460 g
¼ oz	salt		7 g
¼ oz	sugar		7 g
10 oz	milk		300 g
1 oz	egg		30 g
1½ oz	lard		45 g
1 oz	yeast		30 g

Straight dough process at 80°F. Knock back after half an hour and scale after only a further 15 minutes at 1 oz each roll. Mould round and then long (about 2 inches–2½ inches) and place on a warmed, clean and lightly greased tray.

An average egg weighs about 2 oz; this recipe use 1 oz of whole egg, so there will be about 1 oz of whole egg over. This may not be enough to wash them all over but you can try. If not mix another egg into it.

The rolls should be brushed with egg as soon as they are on the tray. Make sure they are spaced out so that they will not touch one another or the side of the tray when proved. Prove them warm, and very carefully brush them a second time with egg just before baking them at 470°F. Take them out when golden-brown. They will not take long at this size.

Fancy Tea Rolls are made from the same dough mixture, but are then weighed at 1½ oz and rolled out to about 9 inches long and tied into several kinds of knots and shapes. Some can be rolled into "C" shapes, others into "S" shapes and yet others are knotted, divided into three and plaited, and so on. There are hundreds of shapes for fancy rolls but don't try anything that can't be done and put on the tray very quickly, for too much time lying about will spoil the shapes and could ruin the dough. Immediately they are on the tray they should be washed with egg to prevent skinning, and again before putting them in the oven. This gives a beautiful gloss, but it must be done with care. Don't let any egg get on the tray, but be sure and wash the roll all over (except for the underneath, of course).

Other rolls of interest are the round ones used for hamburgers and the long ones used for frankfurters (hot dogs). Hamburger rolls are made in the same way as Yorkshire teacakes but using a plainer dough.

Hot Dog Rolls use the same dough as for Hamburger Rolls but rolled out as for Bridge Rolls. Scaling weight for each is 3 oz.

Hamburger Rolls

1 lb 0 oz	flour	460 g
¼ oz	salt	7 g
¼ oz	sugar	7 g
1 oz	lard	30 g
10 oz	milk	300 g
1 oz	yeast	30 g
1 oz	sour dough (optional)	30 g

Straight dough method at 80°F. Ferment for 1 hour. Scale at 3 oz each roll. Mould and shape as required. Prove on warm trays and bake at 480°F. Wash them with milk immediately on taking them from the oven.

Appetizers, Dough Biscuits and Soup Sticks

There are a number of kinds of bread which are deliberately made somewhat drier than most. They compensate for this dryness by always being served with plenty of liquid, usually either with soup at the beginning of a meal, or along with drinks before or after. Being dry they keep longer than ordinary bread, so can be made less often. The wise cook or hostess will always keep one or two varieties of these breads in a tin, to bring out either on the unexpected arrival of guests or just for dipping into. Heat up again just before use.

It is Italy we have to thank for these soup sticks.

Italian Soup Sticks

1 lb 0 oz	flour	460 g
¼ oz	salt	7 g
3 oz	lard	85 g
8 oz	water	230 g
¼ oz	sugar	7 g
1 oz	yeast	30 g
2 oz	sour dough (optional)	60 g

Straight dough, well mixed. Make at 80°F and ferment for 1 hour. Scale at 1 oz each, mould round on to the table, then allow to recover for 10 minutes under a cloth.

For **grissini**, roll them out to about 5 inches long and tray them up on warmed trays. Prove warm, then egg-wash them and bake at 480°F.

For **crissinii**, roll the pieces out to 12 inches long, then roll a slight neck at each end to make the ends like the heads of drumsticks. Then place them on the trays straight as a ruler. Eggwash then prove, and bake at 480°F. They will not take long to bake but do make sure that they are baked fully.

Serve crissinii like celery in a self-service tumbler, to be crunched during soup or broken into it.

Salt Sticks and Rings

1 lb 0 oz	flour	460 g
¼ oz	salt	7 g
1 oz	lard	30 g
7 oz	water	200 g
3 oz	milk	80 g
1 oz	yeast	30 g
2 oz	sour dough (optional)	60 g

Use the straight dough process at 80°F. Ferment for 1 hour then weigh off at ½ oz (yes, ½ oz). Then roll them out into long strips, and make into sticks, rings or open knots. Wash with egg and dip the tops in salt. Tray up, prove, and bake at 430°F.

These are then served in a basket or bowl during drinks. They develop thirst no less than potato crisps but they are quite distinctive. They go down well at cocktail parties, and should always be available on the home bar, along with the cheese sticks and wholemeal sticks mentioned below. The salt sticks are continental, but cheese sticks are much more British.

Cheese Sticks and Rings

1 lb 0 oz	flour	460 g
2 oz	grated cheese (preferably white Stilton)	60 g
¼ oz	sugar	7 g
1 oz	lard	30 g
7 oz	water	200 g
3 oz	milk	80 g
1 oz	yeast	30 g

Straight dough made as for the salt sticks and rings, except after rolling out the tops are washed with egg and dipped in grated cheese. Because the cheese colours well in baking, bake starting at 430°F, then lower the heat to about 400°F. By the way, these are absolutely delicious. If you want to serve them when they are not too fresh, put them back in the oven for a few minutes first.

Add variety by making other thin shapes, and by mixing the salt and cheese ones in a bowl along with the tasty brown rings and sticks as follows:

Wholemeal Sticks

1 lb 0 oz	wholemeal	460 g
2 oz	grated cheese	60 g
1 oz	lard	30 g
¼ oz	salt	7 g
7 oz	water	200 g
3 oz	milk	80 g
1 oz	yeast	30 g

Method exactly as for Cheese Sticks recipe.

Cheese Dough Biscuits

1 lb 0 oz	flour	460 g
3 oz	cheese	90 g
8 oz	milk	200 g
4 oz	lard	110 g
1 oz	yeast	30 g

Make up into a stiff dough. Allow to rest for 1 hour under a damp cloth. The temperature is not so important with these. Then weigh them off at 6 oz, shape them round and cover for 10 minutes. Pin them out to 8-inch circles and cut into eight equal segments. Wash over with diluted egg and dip them each in grated cheese. Place on lightly greased trays, prick well all over with a fork, and allow to recover for 25–30 minutes. Bake at 400°F until a nice golden colour. They taste like small Welsh Rarebits and are lovely fresh.

French Sticks and Rye Bread

Many interesting types of bread are made in the countries of Europe, several of which can be made using the techniques already described.

One of the most popular continental types is the French stick, known in this country often by the un-European and anti-metric name of the yardstick. This is because English bakers often consider the right thickness to be achieved when one pound of dough has been rolled a yard long. French bakers, I am sure, never think in these terms, least of all about their own national bread. Now, it is quite obvious that no one is going to make a French stick a yard long whose oven is not at least as long inside. The maximum length one can make in a domestic oven will be much less spectacular, although the bread itself need not be inferior. The "pound to a yard" formula can still act as a guide to the thickness of the sticks.

Another problem, however, is that French sticks are normally made in a Vienna oven. Apart from putting a bowl of hot water in the bottom of the oven early before baking, and keeping the door shut for the first 10 minutes baking, and then removing the water to finish baking dry, there is not much one can do. Fortunately this gives a pretty good imitation provided the dough is right.

English visitors to France often come back home full of enthusiasm for this bread, but it must be remembered that the French enjoy fresh-tasting bread only because they are prepared to shop for it sometimes several times in one day. French sticks are in fact just about the fastest staling bread there is. The British try too often to make their much better keeping bread do for a week.

French Sticks

1 lb 0 oz	flour	460 g
¼ oz	salt	7 g
¼ oz	sugar	7 g
10 oz	water	300 g
1 oz	yeast	30 g
1 oz	sour dough	30 g
	(optional)	

Straight dough process. Dough temperature 70°F (note that this is quite a *cold* dough). Not too soft. Flatten it out on the table and fold air into it gently every 20 minutes for 2 hours. This helps to build up the uneven, holey texture which is characteristic of this bread.

Divide into two loaves and first mould up lightly as for ordinary tin bread. Allow the dough to recover for a few minutes. Then roll, from the middle outwards with both hands, until each piece is nearly a yard long, and of even width throughout the length. Cut it into pieces the length of your tray, lay on a part of the table dusted with ground rice, and cover until proved.

Ends of French Loaves Proving in Cloths

Basket for Proving Long Loaves

Meanwhile clean the trays, and heat them in the oven, and place the bowl or pan of hot water in the bottom of the oven. (You may find an old cake tin which will do this job well.)

When the loaves are proved, take the trays from the oven and dust them with ground rice. Very carefully (so as not to remove the gas or spoil the shape) place the loaves on the hot rice. Space them so they will not touch, and keep them straight. Make parallel diagonal cuts with a razor blade every 2–3 inches, then quickly put the hot trays back into the steamy oven at about 480°F. Bake and cook as usual and eat shortly afterwards. They can be cut lengthways to make colossal sandwiches, but are more usually buttered at the end and broken by hand.

Rye Bread

There are many different types of rye bread, ranging from light tea bread types to heavy, rich dark and strong breads. At one time considerable quantities of rye bread were eaten in Great Britain, but today it is regarded as something more exotic than it really is to us. For this reason it is not easy to get hold of rye flour, and when you do you can't often specify a certain type, but have to take what comes. Because of this the recipe given has been designed to suit pretty well all kinds of rye flour.

Rye will make gluten when made into dough, just as wheat will. But with rye there is neither as much, nor is it as strong. For this reason we often use a quantity of wheat flour as well to help it along. Rye can be a bit dry, and to counteract this while building good flavour we usually wet the rye in a soft sponge early on so that it gets a good long wetting. Because the gluten in rye dough tends to be sticky, the dough is made quite stiff compared with wheat breads. Further, because of its closer texture and greater heaviness it requires a longer baking at a lower temperature than bread made only with wheat.

The sour dough, mentioned frequently in other recipes as an optional extra, is more than ever required when making rye bread. Use an ordinary white bread sour, but do not afterwards put rye bread into it. By this stage the use of sour dough has probably become habitual in plain breads. Good.

Rye sour			
3 oz	rye flour	85 g
2 oz	water (cold)	60 g
1 oz	sour dough	30 g

Mix well and then leave in a polythene container covered with a damp cloth for 24 hours at 80°F or thereabouts.

Dough			
6½ oz	rye flour	185 g
6½ oz	white flour	185 g

¼ oz	salt	7 g
1 oz	yeast	30 g
1 oz	caraway seeds	30 g
11 oz	water	310 g

Dough temperature 80°F. Make up with the rye sour (above) included. The best way to get the caraway seeds in is to crush them with the rolling pin along with the salt just to break them down a bit before mixing both through the flours.

Knock back after 40 minutes and divide into two loaves at 1 hour after kneading. Mould the loaves up as for tin bread but then just prove and bake them spaced out on a flat tray. Prove well, warm and in a moist atmosphere. Make diagonal parallel razor-blade cuts into the top surface, and place in an oven with plenty of steam as with the French sticks. Baking temperature 440°F.

When half-baked they can be brushed over with a wash made from ½ pint of water and 1 oz of flour. For this the ounce of flour is mixed with just enough of the water to just wet it to a smooth paste. The remainder of the water is boiled and poured boiling onto the flour paste. Stir vigorously as with cornflour custard. This "scald" can be made well in advance and used hot or cold. Brush it over the crust of the half-baked loaves then pop them back to finish. Or after brushing them scatter a few caraway seeds along the middle of the top before replacing the loaves. (If you don't like caraway seeds — and, however marvellous the flavour, they do look and feel like fingernails — leave them out. Or for flavour slip them in the grinder for a few seconds first.) By the way, you may find this scald improves your French sticks too. The French bakers wouldn't do it, but in the more Eastern parts of Europe it is more common. Rye bread is anyway associated mainly with Eastern Europe.

The above recipe can be varied a little by using sour milk instead of water in the rye sour part. Or try adding up to 1 oz black treacle to the dough part. Or both.

Try 1 oz malt extract, or honey, in the dough in place of the treacle just suggested. And if you wish you could add up to ½ oz of your favourite herbs and/or spices.

By experimenting in this way, you will eventually produce your own distinctive rye loaf which suits your own taste.

Hotplate Breads

"Oh, do you know the muffin man,
the muffin man, the muffin man,
do you know the muffin man
who lives in Crumpet Lane?"

Traditional

If you are fortunate enough to have a hotplate or griddle on your cooker, you can make a whole range of hotplate breads. Probably the most famous of these is the English muffin. Until quite recently they were sold in many public places from a hand cart by the local muffin-man. I think the last muffin-man worked in the Brontë sisters' village of Haworth until only a few years ago, pushing his cart up and down the steep main street and ringing a large hand bell to accompany his shout of "Muffins!"

The muffin is one of the most English of specialities, and it is a pity so few real muffins are made today. It is presumed that they originated in London, although they are now made all over the country, being made larger in the north of England than the south. A good muffin should be square at the edges, a beautiful chestnut-brown colour, with white sides and a light, soft texture inside. They should be 1–1½ inches thick.

Muffins

1 lb 0 oz	strong white flour	460 g
¼ oz	salt	7 g
½ oz	sugar or honey	15 g
10 oz	water	300 g
½ oz	cooking oil	15 g
½ oz	yeast	15 g

Straight dough method. Dough temperature 82°F. Use a little extra water if necessary to make a very slack dough and toughen it well with very thorough kneading. Bulk fermentation time 2 hours. Knock-back after 80 minutes. Weigh off at 2½ oz. Using a dough as soft (or slack) as this, moulding is something of a knack. Best results seem to be obtained if, instead of coating them in dusting flour, you dip your hands in a little warm water between moulding and shape up the pieces in the hands instead of on the table. Prove on a tea-towel dusted with ground rice. Care must be taken to keep them warm throughout proof, and to avoid drying or crusting of the top.

The heat of the hotplate is a matter of experience. A teacher of mine used to say if you put your finger on the hotplate, it is ready when you get a smell of roast pork! A safer method is to dust the plate with a little white flour. It should go brown after about 2½ minutes.

When fully proved, drop the muffins straight on to the clean, lightly greased hotplate. Being so soft they will partially flatten on loading. Turn them over when the bottoms are nicely brown, using a palette knife or steel paint-scraper. When they are fully coloured on both sides, it is a good idea to turn them again for a little in order to be sure they are cooked right through. There are few things worse than a half-baked muffin, with its characteristic collapsing sides and hard centre core of dough.

When ready, muffins should not be cut, but like dinner rolls broken open with the fingers before filling with butter and cheese, ham, preserves, or what you like.

They can, of course, be made also using wholemeal flour, substituting treacle for honey. If the wholemeal flour is not very strong substituting, say, 2 oz strong white flour for 2 oz of the wholemeal will help you to make lighter muffins.

Crumpets or Pikelets

For these you will need some proper metal crumpet rings, usually 3½ inches in diameter. Also it takes a little experimenting to adjust the fermentation time and temperature, the consistency, and temperature of the latter (not to mention that of the hotplate too!) in order to get them nicely covered with deep holes.

Crumpets

1 lb 0 oz	strong white flour	460 g
½ oz	yeast	15 g
¼ oz	salt	7 g
1 lb 6 oz	water at 90°F	650 g
½ oz	honey	15 g
½ oz	vegetable oil	15 g

Mix the yeast and honey into the water, add the oil and flour and whisk well. Put in a warm place in a bowl until it rises and drops. Then scrape down and stir to knock the gas out.

Clean and grease the hotplate and rings. Place the rings on the hotplate and pour in enough batter to half-fill each ring. There should not be too much grease on the plate.

It is a good idea to try one or two to make sure the consistency is not too stiff to pour or too soft to cook properly. If they are right, carry on until all the batter is used. When the edges are cooked and set, the rings can be taken off. Finally, when the top has holed and dried, turn them over just to colour the tops a little. Then take them off. They are usually served toasted and hot, with butter melted into the holes.

Baking-powder Crumpets

1 lb 0 oz	white flour	460 g
1 oz	baking powder	30 g
2 oz	nut oil	60 g
2 oz	egg (1 egg)	60 g
6 oz	castor sugar	170 g
⅛ oz	salt	4 g
1 lb 12 oz	milk (cold)	800 g

Cream the sugar, oil, salt and egg in a basin. Add half the milk and whisk to a batter with the flour and baking powder. Whisk in the remaining milk, allow to stand just about 5 minutes, then cook on the hotplate just as the recipe above.

Powder Breads

When making bread with yeast a loaf with particular characteristics is produced, because yeast fermentation does several other things to a dough besides pushing gas into it. While very acceptable bread can be made using baking powder instead of yeast, a totally different process must be used, producing a different kind of bread. Baking-powder breads are of fairly recent date, for baking powder was invented in the port of Bristol as a substitute for yeast for making bread on board ship. The idea was used in the Navy at a time before the preservation of yeast over long voyages was possible.

Baking powder is a mixture of two chemicals. Bicarbonate of soda produces the gas, and an acid is used with it to neutralize the soda and so prevent a taste of soapiness and discoloration.

Since there is no fermentation by yeast it is necessary to use a lot more liquid than for "ordinary" bread to soften the gluten. Further, part of the ripening is done either by using buttermilk (the sour milk left over after churning off butter) or sour milk, or by making a lactic batter.

All the dry ingredients are fully mixed with the fat in a bowl, then the cold liquid is poured in and quickly and lightly stirred.

In fact the method is as near as you like the opposite of that used for the yeast breads. Why? Because we do not want a tough gluten to mature, as there will be no maturing (fermentation) time. Also, if the dough is not cold, and put in the oven quite quickly, the gas will be spent. Unlike yeast, chemical powders only supply a fixed quantity of gas. Any gas supplied before baking is therefore lost lightness.

Another way of helping to prevent toughness due to unfermented gluten is to use an all-purpose flour instead of a bread flour. The addition of a little sour dough will help as well, provided it is very thoroughly mixed through the milk before the dough is made up.

The following dough can be baked in a round or long bread tin.

Powder Bread

Solid mix	1 lb 0 oz	flour	460 g
	¼ oz	salt	7 g
	1 oz	baking powder	30 g
	1 oz	lard	30 g
Liquid part	13 oz	milk	380 g
	1 oz	honey or syrup	30 g
	1 oz	sour dough	30 g

Rub the salt, baking powder and lard through the flour in a bowl, making sure that they are all thoroughly mixed.

Dissolve the honey or golden syrup in the milk, and break the sour dough through them. This liquid should be mixed at least an hour before the dough, and cold, 3 or 4 hours would be better, and milk that is beginning to go sour is best.

The cold liquid is then all poured into the flour mix and very quickly stirred until mixed. There must be *no* kneading, stretching or tearing. Divide the mix into two equal pieces, shape them gently on a floured board, and drop them into greased tins. Dust the tops with a little flour, and cut long loaves once the full length, and round ones twice to make a cross. Pop straight in an oven at 420°F with a bowl of water below for steam. Bake carefully for about 40 minutes. Cool as usual before use.

Alternatively the scone-round shape could be baked on a tray by flattening it slightly before cutting. When made in this way they are known as farls and large numbers of them are made in Scotland and Ireland, moistened with buttermilk.

Just to give an idea of the time taken to prepare this dough, after mixing the dry ingredients in one bowl and the liquid in another, and preparing the tins and the oven, I timed the mixing, dividing, shaping, tinning, to closing the oven door on them. The total time was 1 minute 50 seconds. They are bound to look "rough and country" so the shaping is not as important as the speed.

If you pin the round loaves out flat just under 1 inch thick and then cut them into four, the quarters, or farls can be cooked on a hot plate on both sides, or cooked in a *little* lard in a frying pan.

Wholemeal Soda Bread

1 lb 0 oz	wholemeal	460 g
¼ oz	salt	7 g
1 oz	baking powder	30 g
1 oz	lard	30 g
13 oz	milk	380 g
1 oz	treacle	30 g
1 oz	sour dough	30 g

Method is exactly as for Powder Bread.

While powder breads are very much enjoyed by some people, for many of us they are emergency substitutes for what we think of as real bread. However, the same process used with a much richer kind of mixing will produce a range of afternoon tea breads absolutely second to none, especially where fruit of some kind is added. When adding fruit to a powder bread, it should go into the solid or dry mix after the rest of the dry ingredients have been rubbed together. In this way it gets mixed throughout without the mixing time being extended.

Rich Powder Bread

Solid mix	1 lb 0 oz	flour	460 g
	¼ oz	salt	7 g
	1 oz	baking powder	30 g
	2 oz	butter or lard	60 g

Liquid mix	11 oz	milk	320 g
	2 oz	egg (1 egg)	60 g
	2 oz	honey or syrup	60 g
	1 oz	sour dough	30 g

Method as for Powder Bread. Bake in a cooler oven at 400°F–410°F. A rich brown can be made using wholemeal instead of white flour. Either can be dusted with flour before cutting or brushed with egg just afterwards.

The same recipes are used for **Fruit Soda Breads** using up to a maximum of 5 oz (145 g) of fruit to this mix. Currants, sultanas, raisins, cut dates, cut cherries (not whole), ¼ inch cubes of dried prunes or dried apricots, broken walnuts, or any combination of these will do. Try cherry and ginger, using 4 oz cut cherries and adding ¼ oz ground ginger to the solid mix. Or better still 1 oz of cubed crystallized ginger with the cherries.

The same fruit mixings can be weighed at 6 oz, shaped round, cut in quarters about ½ inch thick and cooked on a hotplate or in the frying-pan, or washed with egg and baked on trays with or without turning when half-done. Or treat as for scones and make some super tea scones.

Alternatively, without fruit, cook in deep fat with a hole in the middle of rings just as we did with doughnuts. Some people prefer these to yeasted doughnuts. Try and see. . . .

Once again, they can all be made using wholemeal flour in place of white flour.

But how about Oaten Cake for a Powder Bread with a difference?

Tasty Oaten Cake

Solid mix	8 oz	flour	230 g
	4 oz	wholemeal	115 g
	4 oz	medium oatmeal	115 g
	¼ oz	salt	7 g
	1 oz	baking powder	30 g
	1 oz	lard	30 g
Liquid mix	13 oz	milk	380 g
	1 oz	treacle	30 g
	1 oz	sour dough	30 g

Method the same as for Powder Bread. Dust with oatmeal before baking at 420°F.

Special Breads

Some of the most unusual-sounding breads are among the most enjoyable, and among these can be counted tomato bread and cheese bread. Both of these are ideal for serving at breakfast plain, fried or toasted, and as a base for cocktail sandwiches along with more ordinary breads.

Tomato Bread

1 lb 0 oz	flour	460 g
¼ oz	salt	7 g
½ oz	sugar	15 g
1 oz	yeast	30 g
2 oz	tomato purée	60 g
½ oz	lard	15 g
10 oz	milk (approx.)	300 g
1 oz	sour dough (optional)	30 g

Straight dough method at 80°F. The dough is fermented for 1 hour before dividing into two tin loaves. It will rise well, and can be washed over after baking with milk as with milk bread. A little pink colour can be added to the milk just to accentuate the tomato colour slightly, especially for cocktail sandwiches. The dough can be made into soft rolls if desired, or by adding another 2 oz flour, 2½ oz lard and ½ oz tomato ketchup it can be worked off exactly as the crissinii into tomato sticks and served in a glass for crunching at cocktail parties.

Sliced for sandwiches, tomato bread can be alternated with layers of cheese bread to give colour and flavour combinations that will delight your friends. The cheese bread is made in just the same way.

Cheese Bread

1 lb 0 oz	flour	460 g
¼ oz	salt	7 g
½ oz	sugar	15 g
1 oz	yeast	30 g
3 oz	grated Cheddar cheese	85 g
½ oz	lard	15 g
10 oz	milk (approx.)	300 g
1 oz	sour dough (optional)	30 g

The method is exactly the same as for Tomato Bread. The milk quantity may need adjusting because cheese varies in dryness. It ought to be very finely grated and well mixed in, and there is a notable improvement in flavour if, instead of a straight dough, a sponge and no-time dough process is used as with the milk bread. If you wish to try this, just take all the milk, yeast, sugar and cheese and 6 oz of the flour for a 1-hour sponge, and add everything else at the dough stage. Knead very thoroughly and *tin up* straight away.

For a change how about corn bread? Corn, or maize, originated in America. It is the main part of the diet of millions of people in the more tropical areas where wheat will not grow well. It is used in England for making cornflour (corn starch) and maize oil, breakfast cereals, and animal feeds.

In parts of Ireland a form of scone is made called golden drop, and farls are cooked on the hotplate, called Indian farls. Both are made using yellow maize instead of wheat flour, with a process similar to that described under Powder Breads.

In Italy a kind of porridge is made from corn meal, called polenta, and is the main part of the diet of many of the poorer people. But corn breads are usually unleavened and quite gritty, due to the fact that maize protein will not form gluten. To produce a loaf with any lightness it is necessary to use quite a lot of white wheat flour to provide the gluten, and even then not to expect the bread to be quite as light as a white loaf.

Lightness, however, isn't everything. By getting the right consistency and full control over the fermentation it can be made as light as possible. The different texture, the spotted crust, the bright colour, and the unusual flavour all help to make corn bread an interesting addition to the repertoire of any cook.

Corn Bread

11 oz	flour	330 g	
5 oz	yellow maize	150 g	
¼ oz	salt	7 g	
¼ oz	lard	7 g	
¼ oz	sugar	7 g	
1 oz	yeast	30 g	
10 oz	milk (approx.)	300 g	

Straight dough method at 80°F. One hour to dividing into two loaves in tins or on trays. Before putting the proved loaves in the oven, especially if they are to be baked on trays (for which moulding "boat shape" is particularly appropriate) brush them over with cooled corn wash. This is made by stirring a little out of ½ pint of water into 2 oz yellow maize, boiling the remainder and making a "scald". Allow to cool and then stir in 1 egg yolk and a pinch of salt.

Now if you can make a special kind of bread with a cereal other than wheat, and one which cannot make gluten, the fact itself will open up possibilities for many other kinds of bread.

In fact you can substitute up to about one-third of white flour with another cereal and still get reasonable aeration, provided care is taken with times and temperatures throughout. One of the pleasantest breads of this type is probably the oaten bread.

Oaten Bread

10 oz	flour	290 g
6 oz	medium oatmeal	170 g
¼ oz	salt	7 g
½ oz	lard	15 g
½ oz	treacle or golden syrup	15 g
1 oz	yeast	30 g
10 oz	water	300 g

Straight dough process with 1 hour to scaling at 80°F. Divide into two loaves. Shape round. Flatten slightly. Brush the tops with warm water and dip in oatmeal for a nice homely finish. Prove and bake at 460°F on lightly greased trays.

This bread is quite light and tasty. A stronger-flavoured loaf can be made which has a most appealing flavour in what I call a "heavy oaten bread". This should be sliced thinly and eaten with cheese, preferably a good white Stilton. If the bread is wrapped in foil after cooling it will keep for over a week, and will be pleasanter to eat one or two days after baking.

Rolled oats (porridge oats) can be used instead of oatmeal, but, believe me, it is not the same either for flavour or texture. And oatmeal *can* be bought if you pester your grocer or delicatessen.

Heavy Oaten Bread

10 oz	flour	300 g
6 oz	fine oatmeal	170 g
¼ oz	salt	7 g
1½ oz	lard	45 g
1½ oz	treacle	45 g
½ oz	malt extract or honey	15 g
1 oz	yeast	30 g
2 oz	egg (1 egg)	60 g
10 oz	milk	300 g
	a pinch of ginger	
2 oz	sour dough	60 g
	(optional but desirable)	

Straight dough process as for oaten bread. This is better baked *under* two 1 lb loaf tins. Try greasing the tins and then dusting them with oatmeal and tipping out any surplus. Or use this mix for plant-pot bread. Prove them fairly well up because they won't rise very much in the oven. Bake at 400°F slowly and fully.

If you like them, try also adding 1 oz caraway seeds. Everybody calls them caraway seeds, but in fact they are not seeds at all, they are the dried fruits of a plant of the parsley family. They act as a stimulant to the digestion. Caraways are used in perfumery, as a flavour for cordials in liqueurs such as Aquavit and Kummel, in European rye breads and some continental cheeses and soups. They were frequently used in breads and cakes in this country until the last century, and are still used quite a lot in some parts of Ireland. The use of caraway "seeds" in bread, therefore, is something which has been extremely popular in the past.

Caraway Bread

1 lb 0 oz	flour		460 g
¼ oz	salt		7 g
½ oz	sugar		15 g
½ oz	fat		15 g
7 oz	water		210 g
3 oz	milk		90 g
1 oz	yeast		30 g
3 oz	caraway seeds		90 g

Straight dough method at 80°F. One hour to scaling. Add the caraway seeds in at the first mixing, either as they come or crushed a bit, or put through the grinder. (If you grind them you will need to increase the milk because of the extra dry powder in the mixing.)

The same recipe can be made up using half or all wholemeal flour. Or if you just like a little caraway flavour, drop a few caraways (whole or ground) in the oaten bread (Tomato Bread page 123, and Cheese Bread page 124).

One of the most luxurious British breads is Honey Tea Bread, which should rise so well that it will fill two large loaf tins when baked *under* them. For teatime it is beautiful both for lightness and flavour, with a soft texture and a beautiful thin golden crust. It keeps well, and slices easily, and if allowed to survive uneaten for a week will still make super toast.

Honey Tea Bread

1 lb 0 oz	flour	460 g
¼ oz	salt	7 g
1½ oz	butter	45 g
1½ oz	honey	45 g
2 oz	egg (1 egg)	60 g
9 oz	milk	260 g
1 oz	yeast	30 g

Straight dough, soft, at 80°F. One hour to dividing into two loaves. Shape long and place on a clean, warmed, greased tray. Prove *under* two large loaf tins for half an hour if at 80°F (a bit longer if cooler), then bake off for 35–40 minutes at 400°F.

Dough Cakes are made by taking half of the tin-bread dough (see page 48) after fermenting it and making the other half into a tin loaf, and mixing in 4 oz sugar, 8 oz butter, 8 oz eggs, 1 oz of your favourite spices, and 1 lb 4 oz of any dried fruit. The fruit should be left out until the mixture is smooth, and then mixed through evenly. Divide into two or three cakes of equal size, shape and proof for over an hour before baking at 400°F or slightly less. Brush the tops with butter after baking.

Savarins, Babas, Brioches and Butter Croissants

The best of the fermented lines from France are included here, in small size mixes.

Brioches

8 oz	flour		240	g
⅛ oz	salt		4	g
½ oz	sugar		15	g
½ oz	yeast		15	g
4½ oz	egg		135	g
4½ oz	butter		135	g

Make a very stiff dough with all ingredients except a little of the egg and all the butter. Knead very thoroughly then place the dough in a deep bowl or bucket half to three-quarters full of water (at 80°F). The dough will sink to the bottom of the bucket, but will float on the surface when it is ready to take. This is the traditional way to do it. Take it out and let most of the water drip off it.

Then work in the rest of the eggs, and afterwards chop through the butter. Work this thoroughly until smooth, put in a bowl and place in the refrigerator or in a cold place for an hour to stiffen the butter (otherwise they are too sticky to handle). Weigh off at 1 oz and shape round, and place in well-greased, clean cupcake tins. Prove. Eggwash, and bake at 450°F. Or they can be assembled in these tins like little tiny cottage loaves to make a novel shape. Some people decorate them just before putting them in the oven by giving two or three snips with a pair of clean scissors.

Be careful not to overbake them as they should be very moist and light.

Butter Croissants

8 oz	flour	240 g
⅛ oz	salt	4 g
½ oz	sugar	15 g
½ oz	yeast	15 g
5 oz	milk	150 g
4 oz	butter	120 g

Make a dough with all except the butter. Allow dough to rest for half an hour, then pin it out to a square about 10 inches (25 cm) and spread the butter over a diamond shape, touching all four sides in the middle. Fold the butter in by making the dough into an envelope. Seal it well in, then roll out the dough to about 12 inches by 6 inches and fold into three. Try not to fold in dusting flour. Turn 90° (i.e. from 12.00 to 3.15) and repeat. Cover and allow to lie for a further half-hour. Then pin out, fold into three and turn three times more and allow another half-hour to recover.

Pin out to ⅛ inch thick and cut into 6 inch strips. Out of each strip cut 4 inch wide triangles, and roll each one so that the point comes down in the middle. Roll them fairly lightly and seal the point down, then turn to a crescent shape and place on warmed, lightly greased trays. Eggwash and prove nicely before baking at 470°F. Be careful not to prove them too hot or the butter will melt and spoil the flaky texture of these lovely goodies. They can be served with coffee as a continental breakfast, as can the brioche just described. Or serve with soup. Or for tea. Or just eat them anytime you want, they are beautiful and light and you can taste the butter.

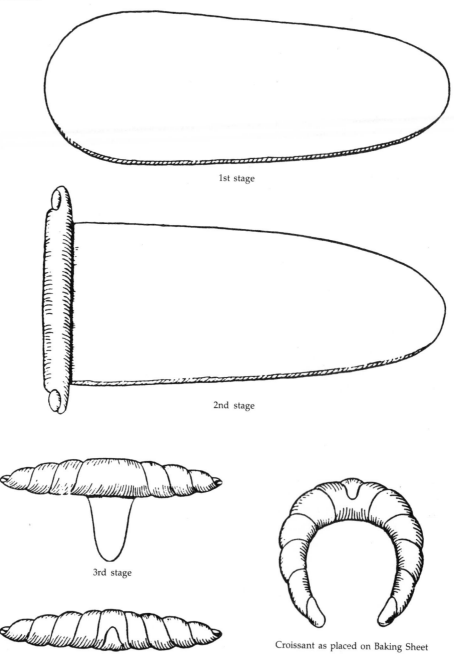

1st stage

2nd stage

3rd stage

4th and final stage

Croissant as placed on Baking Sheet

Stages in Moulding a Roll

Baba au Rhum

8 oz	flour	240	g
½ oz	sugar	15	g
4 oz	eggs	120	g
⅛ oz	salt	4	g
½ oz	yeast	15	g
5 oz	milk	140	g
2 oz	butter	60	g
2 oz	currants	60	g

Straight dough method, using everything except currants. Make and keep the dough at 80°F. The dough should be soft. Add the currants after 40 minutes' proof, then allow the dough another 20 minutes' rest. Divide into eight, shape up round, and drop into well-greased, clean individual pie cases, patty cases, or cupcake tins. Prove fully and bake at 470°F.

When baked, cool them upside-down on a wire, then soak them in syrup. The syrup for these, and for the savarins, is made from 4 oz sugar (120 g) brought to the boil in 10 oz water (300 g) with a bay leaf, the rind and juice of one lemon, two or three coriander seeds and half a stick of cinnamon. Allow this to cool and then strain and add 2 oz rum.

Put the syrup in a basin, and soak the cooled babas well in it. Put them on a wire and brush them all over with boiled, strained apricot jam. Allow to cool then pipe a whirl of whipped fresh cream on top and decorate with *glacé* cherries and a couple of diamonds of angelica. Serve as a sweet course at dinner.

The **Savarin** is made with exactly the same dough except without the currants. The above mixing will make two and for them you will need two savarin tins. These are shaped like a car tyre so that the finished savarins are like quoits, only thicker. Dip them and soak well in the syrup when they are cool, then brush with boiled strained apricot jam. Place on a serving-dish and fill the centre with fruit salad (without juice — the juice can go in the syrup instead of sugar and water if you are using a tinned fruit salad or fruit cocktail). Decorate with whipped fresh cream and add *glacé* cherries and angelica diamonds to give colour. Serve as a sweet course at dinner.

Flat Breads

One of the main aims in producing acceptable bread is lightness. Bread which is not well aerated is more difficult to eat and for most people less enjoyable. Some wholemeal bread is sufficiently solid and heavy as to be real hard work. Unless the cereal used contains gluten-forming proteins (in other words it is either wheat or rye), normal aeration is not possible.

It is possible to produce acceptable bread without aeration, provided it is made quite thin. There are many kinds of traditional bread which are made deliberately thin instead of being aerated. Obvious examples are cream crackers (water biscuits), rye biscuits and pancakes. An interesting one made in Yorkshire out of a sort of wholeoat porridge and cooked on a hotplate is called "clap bread" because it looks like the cow claps seen in the field. Yorkshire people are known to have a way with words!

Chappatis

1 lb 0 oz	chappati flour	480 g
¼ oz	salt	7 g
½ oz	oil	15 g
9–10 oz	cold water	270–300 g

Rub the salt and oil into the flour. If chappati flour is not available you can use either wholemeal instead or 12 oz wholemeal to 4 oz white bread flour. Add enough water to make a stiff dough. Mix well and knead thoroughly. Allow to recover for half an hour under a damp cloth.

Prepare a cast-iron frying pan or griddle by heating it well.

Break off pieces of dough about 1½ oz (45 g) each. Mould them round, then pin them out very thin, dusting with flour. Cook in the pan, turning over when half-done. Immediately before use, put them under a very hot grill until they jump. Serve with curries or other Indian dishes.

Tortillas are made in exactly the same way, but using yellow maize meal instead of wheat flour. They are a Mexican bread served with Mexican or South American hot dishes.

Pitta Bread originates among the Arab countries and, while flat, it is made with a fermented dough:

1 lb 0 oz	white bread flour	460 g
¼ oz	salt	7 g
½ oz	oil	15 g
½ oz	yeast	15 g
½ oz	malt extract	15 g
10 oz	warm water	285 g

Mix the flour, salt and oil on the table. In a bowl or measure mix the malt extract and yeast into the warm water. Make a hole in the dry ingredients and pour in the fermenting liquid. Make up into dough, knead well, then allow to ferment for 1 hour under a damp cloth.

Weigh off 1¾ oz (50 g) pieces, mould them round, allow 10 minutes to recover, then pin them out to about 5 inches (12 cm) long and oval in shape. Dust with flour and place on a clean, lightly greased tray. Allow 5–10 minutes to recover and bake in a very hot oven (480°F) for about 8 minutes.

After baking they are split and filled with salad or other fillings. Like most bread if they get a bit "tired" they can be freshened up by toasting.

Clap Bread or Havercakes

8 oz	strong plain flour	240 g
8 oz	fine oatmeal	240 g
¼ oz	salt	7 g
½ oz	yeast	15 g
10 oz	warm milk and water	300 g

Mix in large bowl and set aside to rise for one hour by fire. Put one tbsp of mixture onto hot greased griddle. Smooth with knife and turn to cook both sides. Serve hot or dry on creel.

Pizzas

Pizza literally means "pie". It has become very popular in recent years and is an excellent way to help the family to increase the bread intake without at the same time pushing up the butter, jam and syrup.

Here is a good recipe. Try it and then experiment with toppings.

8 oz	wholemeal flour	240	g
8 oz	white bread flour	240	g
¼ oz	salt	7	g
7 oz	water	210	g
3 oz	olive oil	90	g
1 oz	yeast	30	g

Mix the two flours together with the salt on the table. Make a bay. Mix the yeast in the water and pour it in the bay, followed by the olive oil. Make up into a smooth dough. Cover with a damp cloth and leave to rise for 1 hour, during which the sauce can be prepared.

2 lb 8 oz	onion	240 g
2 oz	olive oil	60 g
1 lb 0 oz	tomatoes (fresh or tinned)	480 g
4 oz	tomato purée	120 g
1 lb 0 oz	Lancashire cheese	480 g

a little salt, pepper,
oregano, basil
and a crushed garlic clove

You can also use tuna fish, olives, anchovy strips, sliced peppers, mushrooms as desired.

Chop up the onions and fry them in the oil until brown, then add the garlic and continue frying for a minute or so. Add the tomatoes, purée, and seasonings, and simmer until the dough is ready. Put the pan into cold water to cool while you prepare the dough.

Divide the dough into two and mould each piece round. Roll out or press each piece to 10–12 inch circles (20–25 cm). Put them on clean, lightly greased trays. Spread half the sauce over each base evenly. Decorate with any additions you like, then rub the cheese between the hands over the top. Lanchashire cheese will not need grating, as it just crumbs down in the hands and makes a pleasant topping for an "anglicized" pizza.

Allow half an hour to prove before baking at 420°F (217°C) for about half an hour. Sniff . . . mmm! Cool on wires.

Plaits and Harvest Festival Breads

Among the most attractive of breads both to look at and to eat are the milk plaits. These are made with a milk bread dough usually made on a straight dough process.

Milk Plait Dough

1 lb 0 oz	flour	460 g
¼ oz	salt	7 g
¼ oz	sugar	7 g
½ oz	lard	15 g
11 oz	milk (approx.)	310 g
1 oz	yeast	30 g

Straight dough process at 80°F. Ferment for 1 hour in bulk then divide into two loaves.

For the three-strand plait, divide one of the loaves into three equal pieces and mould them round. Allow the pieces to recover under a cloth for about 5 minutes; they will hardly need longer as this ought to be a very lively dough. Then roll each piece out with the hands until it is about 10 inches long, thicker in the middle and tapered to the ends. By rolling from the middle out it is possible to roll the gas bubbles out at the two ends and give the strands a firmness which will help the shape of the finished plait. The three pieces ought to be of equal length, size and shape. Plait them from the middle towards yourself, quite tightly, and secure the ends well. Turn the piece right over to do the other ends: in this way any pulling will be the same on each side of the middle.

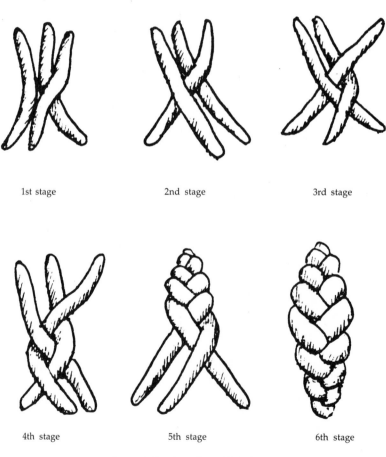

<table>
<tr><td>1st stage</td><td>2nd stage</td><td>3rd stage</td></tr>
<tr><td>4th stage</td><td>5th stage</td><td>6th stage</td></tr>
</table>

Stages in forming a 3 stranded plait

When made up, the piece is placed to prove on a clean, warm, lightly greased tray, and eggwashed both before proof and again just before placing in the oven. If desired you can, after the last eggwashing, scatter over them a few maw seeds (poppy seeds) for decoration and flavour.

It is necessary to work quite quickly when plaiting and traying this bread, since only by doing so can you get a nice bold loaf. The dough is working so quickly that if it is not rolled fairly tightly and plaited straight away it will become loose and poorly shaped. The final shape should be higher and wider in the middle and taper off at each end. Baking temperature is 450°F.

The **Jewish Cholla** is also made in this "baton" shape. For this take off about 3 oz of the dough from one loaf. Shape up the remainder by rolling up as for tin bread and then taper the ends.

Divide the small piece into three and roll each piece out the full length of the loaf, in equal thickness all along. Plait from one end, and stick the long thin plait along the top of the loaf, with a *little* water. Eggwash as with the plait.

In the bakery we are taught how to make plaits of up to about thirteen strands, and many combinations of them to make fancy shapes. The loaves can be very attractive indeed if properly made.

Only the three-strand plait is usually made tapered at the ends. The remainder are divided, moulded, and allowed to recover as above, then rolled out to 10 inch lengths of equal thickness throughout. Stand a weight of some kind over one end, then plait towards yourself tightly. Tidy the two ends then tray, wash, prove, wash again and bake. With a bit of practice many fancy shapes can be developed for this dough.

The milk plaits, if nicely made, can be used for display, such as harvest festivals. However, it is better if possible to make a special festival loaf for such occasions. For with this you can display your skill at moulding with live dough to the full. Your only limitations will be your skill and the size of your oven.

Festival loaves are made on the biggest flat tray you have. The following is a suitable recipe:

Festival Bread

2 lb 0 oz	flour	920 g
½ oz	salt	15 g
¼ oz	sugar	7 g
½ oz	yeast	15 g

13 oz	water	370 g
5 oz	milk	140 g

Take both the water and the milk cold. The dough needs to move slowly so as to give time for moulding the fancy pieces. It should also be quite stiff and requires a very good kneading if it is to look smooth. Being such a stiff dough, it will very readily crust over, so it must be kept moist on the surface.

After mixing, the dough will need 15 minutes to recover. It is then thoroughly re-kneaded and left for a further 15 minutes. Then shape the dough as required on the tray, and put into the oven at 370°F at 2 hours after the end of the first mixing. In order to have a few minutes from completion of the piece to putting it in the oven, therefore, the whole piece needs to be made up in less than 1½ hours. Baking time will vary according to thickness, but will probably be about ¾–1 hour.

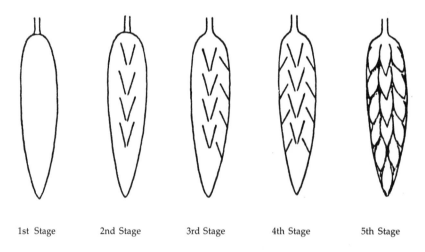

1st Stage   2nd Stage   3rd Stage   4th Stage   5th Stage

After baking, the bread should be cooled on a wire. It can be displayed when fully dry on the crust, and will be fit to look at (although not necessarily to eat!) for just as long as it is kept dry and free from mould and church mice.

The most popular festival loaf is the **Wheatsheaf**. For this the whole dough is first pinned out with a rolling-pin to ½ inch thick. Fold it in half and cut out with a sharp knife the whole shape of the sheaf (a shape like a shaving brush with lather on). This base is opened out as it is placed on a lightly greased, clean, cold tray. Put the rest of the dough under a damp cloth and prick the base right through and all over. Brush it then with water.

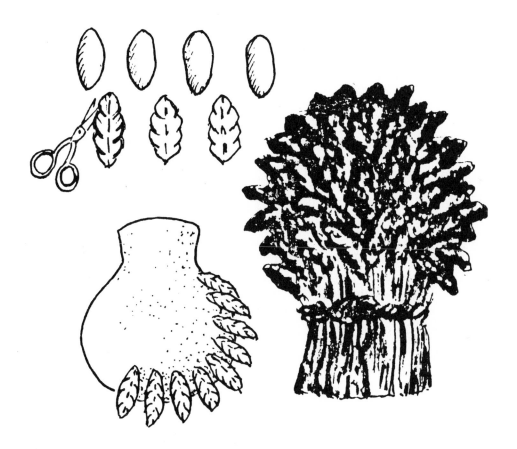

Take about two-thirds of the remainder and divide it roughly into about forty little pieces. Roll them quickly into torpedo shapes and snip each one many times with scissors, always in the same direction. These are placed on the base for ears, starting round the outer edge overlapping on to the tray, and then each overlapping the last, until they are all used up. Each time you stick on two or three, wash them with egg to prevent skinning and if necessary brush the base again with water whenever it gets a bit dry.

When all the ears are on and eggwashed, roll out the remainder of the dough into very thin lengths for stalks. Stick them on close together, as many as possible and as thin as you can. Make the last three strips into a thin plait and strap it over the middle. Eggwash straight away, and again just before putting in the oven.

The **Five Loaves and Two Fishes** loaf is also suitable for harvest festival, and is simpler to make. The base is cut out round or oval, and a frame made with a long narrow plait of dough. Five baby cottage loaves are made and stuck on the well pricked base, and two fishes moulded in the dough, the scales being indicated with scissors, and a currant for each eye. Eggwash and bake.

On the base, within this sort of frame, any amount of other ideas can be modelled using this kind of dough, and you can get much pleasure from developing your own bread sculpture in this way. As festival breads are so traditional in Great Britain I am surprised they appear so rarely on the schedule of the many craft competitions and displays run all over the country every year.

Having taken a brief look at many different kinds of bread, this is a suitable note on which to end. For the craft of breadmaking is one of the oldest and most fascinating. It has been developed over thousands of years, and it is the responsibility of our generation to see that the best of it does not get lost, and if possible that we add something of real value. It is my hope that I have done something in this direction, and that many others will be inspired to learn and to pass on something of this ancient and noble craft.

Good baking, and good eating of good baking!

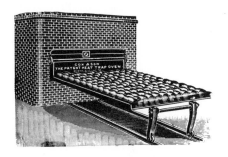

Appendix: British Statistics

Table 1

Estimated Household Consumption of Bread by Type (ounces per person per week)

	1978 oz	1978 %	1980 oz	1980 %	1982 oz	1982 %	1983 oz	1983 %	1984 oz	1984 %	1985 oz	1985 %
Brown	3.15	9.8	4.01	12.9	3.32	10.7	3.18	10.3	3.45	11.3	3.74	12.1
Wholewheat/meal	0.69	2.1	1.55	5.0	2.08	6.7	2.71	8.8	3.12	10.2	3.59	11.6
White large unwrapped	6.31	19.6	5.17	16.6	4.70	15.1	3.99	13.0	3.47	11.3	3.17	10.2
White large wrapped	16.42	51.1	14.53	46.7	15.13	48.7	14.88	48.4	14.82	48.5	14.68	47.4
White small unwrapped	1.88	5.9	1.65	5.3	1.39	4.5	1.46	4.8	1.39	4.5	1.14	3.7
White small wrapped	0.44	1.4	0.52	1.7	0.48	1.6	0.48	1.6	0.37	1.2	0.38	1.2
Others*	3.24	10.1	3.68	11.8	3.94	12.7	4.04	13.1	3.96	13.0	4.29	13.8
TOTAL	32.13	100.0	31.11	100.0	31.04	100.0	30.74	100.0	30.58	100.0	30.99	100.0

* This covers malt bread, french bread, "slimming" bread, white and brown bread rolls. Note the small preference for brown bread which is much lower than most people would guess.
Source: National Food Survey.

Table II

Estimated Household Consumption of Bread by Region (ounces per person per week)

REGION	1969	1976	1977	1978	1980	1982	1983
All Regions	37.74	33.17	32.73	32.13	31.11	31.04	30.74
Wales	43.79	35.74	35.53	38.84	31.89	33.10	32.99
Scotland	42.26	35.24	36.24	38.38	35.15	34.42	34.45
North	42.26	33.85	34.19	34.39	36.75	34.55	35.93
Yorkshire & Humberside	n.a.	31.55	31.95	30.74	29.52	31.88	30.32
North West	40.74	36.21	33.12	33.78	33.32	35.49	31.82
East Midlands	37.40	32.61	32.68	34.97	32.41	31.35	33.08
West Midlands	41.55	38.27	37.95	34.00	33.34	35.22	36.27
South West	34.17	31.47	32.49	30.57	32.42	25.80	27.66
South East & East Anglia	33.67	29.91	29.45	27.58	27.17	27.60	26.69

Source: National Food Survey

Table III

Nutrients Obtained for 1p (1983)

	ENERGY KCAL	PROTEIN	FAT	CARBOHYDRATE	CALCIUM	IRON	THIAMIN	RIBOFLAVIN	NICOTINIC ACID EQUIVALENT
		g	g	g	mg	mg	mg	mg	mg
All Foods	21.44	0.7	1.01	2.5	8.8	0.11	0.01	0.02	0.3
Bread, White (std loaves)	58	2.1	0.4	12.1	26.0	0.38	0.04	0.01	0.6
Bread, Brown and Wholemeal	44	1.8	0.5	8.5	15.5	0.48	0.05	0.02	0.4
Milk*	23	1.1	1.3	1.6	35.5	—	0.01	0.06	0.30
Cheese	18	1.2	1.5	—	35.4	—	—	0.03	0.29
Eggs*	17	1.3	1.3	—	5.9	0.22	0.01	0.06	0.42
Potatoes (old)*	42	0.9	—	9.9	4.6	0.24	0.03	0.02	0.88
Beef and Veal	8	0.6	0.6	—	—	0.07	—	0.01	0.29
Breakfast Cereals	34	0.9	—	7.4	3.3	0.53	0.08	0.11	1.15

* These foods show seasonal variation in nutritional value or price.
  Source: National Food Survey

Table IV

Fibre Content of Bread (large loaves)
% by weight

TYPE	TOTAL DIETARY FIBRE
White	4.1
Brown	6.1
Wholemeal	8.0

Source: Wenlock *et al* 1983

Glossary

Absorption: The maximum amount of water that a particular flour will take in order to produce a dough of suitable consistency.

Baking: Cooking inside a closed oven in which the goods are completely surrounded by heated air.

Bashing: Forcing the first two fingers of each hand through the top and bottom pieces of a cottage loaf, so fixing the two parts of the dough so they do not separate during proof and baking. Shaping of cottage loaf.

Batter: A semi-liquid mixture having the consistency of pouring custard, made primarily with milk or water and flour.

Bay: A pile of dry ingredients on the table, with a hole in the middle big enough to take the liquid.

Bloom: The wholesome appearance naturally seen in the crust colour of a well fermented loaf.

Bloomer: Traditional London crusty loaf baked on rice flour. (An old London expert once told me it should have fourteen diagonal cuts on top.)

Bold loaf: One having good volume and shape.

Bonnet: A metal cover under which individual loaves are baked to give better humidity and more even baking in the oven.

Bound: Too stiff and therefore lacking in volume. Unable to rise freely.

Bran: The outer coverings or skins of cereals. There are actually more than six distinct layers combined in the form "bran".

Bread: A mixture of ground cereals and water cooked solid.

Brioche: A continental light fermented cake, often eaten for breakfast with coffee.

Bulk fermentation time (BFT): The time from dough mixing to dividing and moulding.

Buns: Small breads made with dough enriched with extra fat, sugar, milk, egg, spices and fruit, or various combinations of these extra ingredients.

Bunspice: A mixture of spices specifically blended by flavour manufacturers for addition to Hot Cross Buns.

Bunwash: A liquid used to glaze buns; usually a sugar and water syrup.

Caramel: A syrup made by boiling sugar and water until it begins to brown. Used to add colour and flavour to brown breads, along with or instead of treacle.

Caramelization: When sugar and water are boiled together the water evaporates as the temperature rises; caramelization is what happens when the syrup goes brown.

Casein: The main protein in milk. Casein solidifies when milk sours, due to the action of lactic acid on it.

Cholla: A Jewish bread, baton-shaped and often plaited, eggwashed and decorated with maw seeds (poppy seeds).

Clearing: The complete mixing and smoothing of all ingredients during dough-making.

Consistency: The feel of the dough, used as a measure of water absorption.

Cores: Hard areas in the crumb, recognized by pressing the thumbs on the crumb surface of a cut loaf.

Cornmeal: Another word for maize flour.

Crissinii: Italian soup sticks made from long thin ropes of bread dough with little knobs at each end rather like drumsticks.

Croissant: A traditional continental crescent-shaped roll made by rolling butter into a fermented dough.

Crumb: All the loaf except the crust.

Crust: The outside of the loaf that has dried and caramelized (coloured brown) during baking.

Diastase: Combination of enzymes that convert starch into sugars during fermentation.

Dough: A mixture of flour and water, in which gluten is formed; of a consistency suitable for making bread.

Eggwash, to: To brush with egg.

Elasticity: The quality of a dough to try to spring back to its original shape following handling, especially during moulding.

Endosperm: The part of the wheat grain provided to feed the new plant until the new root can draw food from the soil. The central and white 85 per cent of the grain.

Enzyme: An organic catalyst. A substance that assists in a chemical change without itself being changed.

Extensibility: The degree to which a dough may be stretched without breaking.

Fermentation: An organic chemical change caused by micro-organisms.

Ferment: A liquid medium containing yeast and yeast food or flour, at a suitable temperature to start fermentation.

Flavour: The total combination of taste, aroma and mouth-touch when bread is taken in the mouth.

Flour: Cereal which has been ground into powder.

Foxy colour: The red-brown crust colour which indicates bread made from underfermented dough.

Germ (or embryo): That part of the wheat which begins to grow when the wheat seed falls into the ground. It consists of about 2 per cent of the grain, and is particularly rich in oil, protein and vitamins.

Germ meal: Strong white flour to which has been added at least 12 per cent cooked, salted wheatgerm. Best quality traditional germ bread would contain 75 per cent strong white flour and 25 per cent cooked salted germ. However, such proportions are very expensive, and because of the high oil content a flour of this kind does not keep for more than about two weeks at most.

Gluten: The insoluble protein of wheat or rye flour after being mixed with water. Gluten holds in gas and by stretching during fermentation enables the bread to rise.

Grissini: Italian rolls made about 3 inches (7½ cms) long, moulded straight like sausages.

Invertase: The enzyme in yeast which turns sugar in the dough into a simpler form known as invert sugar, which can then be digested by the yeast.

Knock-back: Re-mixing the dough about two-thirds of the way through the bulk fermentation time.

Lactic batter: A liquid mixture based on milk, in which the partial souring of the milk softens dough and plays a part in flavour development.

Lactose: The natural sugar present in milk. It cannot be fermented by yeast, and so in bread it darkens the crust colour and adds sweetness.

Leaven: Originally a piece of old dough used to start fermentation in a new mixture. The term is now used to indicate any form of yeast addition to dough, such as compressed yeast, a ferment, barm, or other brew.

Loaf: The bread in its final baked shape.

No-time dough: A dough made without bulk fermentation; that is, one mixed, kneaded and divided without any rest time in between.

Oatmeal: Flour made by grinding oats to a powder.

Oven spring: The difference in size between a loaf entering the oven and on completion of the baking.

Poppy seeds: Known also as maw seeds. Used as a decoration on the tops of some speciality breads and rolls.

Proof: The aeration by yeast of any bread or fermented item immediately before baking.

Prover: A cabinet in which it is possible to create ideal (or at least improved) conditions for proof. In a prover the concern will therefore be to control the temperature and humidity of the atmosphere around the goods.

Recovery: When dough is handled, as in moulding or other manipulation, the gluten toughens up and the dough tightens. It is then necessary to let it rest or "recover" for a time, so that it can soften up again, before further handling.

Savarin: A light fermented cake soaked in rum-flavoured sugar syrup and served with fruit and cream. Named after an eighteenth-century cookery writer.

Scale-off: Divide by weight.

Sheen: Reflection of light from the cells in the cut surface of the crumb.

Skin: If dough is exposed to draughts or to a dry atmosphere, the surface will form a most undesirable crust called a skin.

Skimming: To take material off the surface of a liquid, as in skimming cream off milk.

Soda bread: Bread popular in Ireland and Scotland, aerated with bicarbonate of soda instead of yeast.

Sponge: A mixture of flour, water, yeast and possibly other yeast food, allowed to ferment for anything up to 24 hours before being mixed with the rest of the ingredients to form dough. The "old-fashioned" method of making light, flavoursome bread from very strong flour.

Straight dough method: Breadmaking process in which all the ingredients are mixed together at the dough-making stage.

Streaks: Patches in the crumb structure.

Sucrose: Sugar made from sugar cane and sugar beet, although also contained in many other plants.

Wash: Brush over to give a thin liquid coating to the goods in order to enhance their appearance.

Weigh off: Scale off.

Wheatgerm: See germ above.

White flour: Ground endosperm.

Wholemeal: The whole of the wheat ground into four. Legally 95–100 per cent of the grain.

Yield: The number or amount produced.

Zymase: The enzyme in yeast which changes invert sugar into carbon dioxide gas and alcohol. The gas is what lifts the loaf.

Bibliography

W. Banfield: *Manna*, Applied Science Publishers Ltd.

Bateman and Maisner: *The Sunday Times Book of Real Bread*, Rodale Press Ltd.

Edmund Bennion: *Breadmaking, its Principles and Practice*, Oxford University Press.

A. R. Daniels: *A Baker's Dictionary*, Applied Science Publishers Ltd.

A. R. Daniels: *Bakery Materials and Methods*, Applied Science Publishers Ltd.

Elizabeth David: *English Bread and Yeast Cookery*, Penguin Books Ltd. (A. Lane)

Fance and Wragg: *Up-to-date Breadmaking*, Applied Science Publishers Ltd.

L. J. Hanneman: *Breadmaking and Fermented Goods*, William Heinemann Ltd.

Horspool and Geary: *Towards Better Bread*, National Association of Master Bakers.

Kent-Jones and Mitchell: *The Practice and Science of Breadmaking*, Northern Publishing Co. Ltd.

National Association of Master Bakers: *The Master Bakers' Book of Breadmaking*, National Association of Master Bakers.

Sheppard and Newton: *The Story of Bread*, Routledge and Kegan Paul.

Arnold Spicer (ed.): *Bread: Social, Nutritional and Agricultural Aspects of Wheaten Bread*, Applied Science Publishers Ltd.

V. Richter: *Vienna Bread and Continental Breads De Luxe*, Applied Science Publishers Ltd.

A. Williams (ed.): *Breadmaking: The Modern Revolution*, Hutchinson Benham.

Index

Notes

Notes

Notes

Notes

Notes

Notes

Notes